CRY OF THE WILD

Cry of the Wild

Eight animals under siege

CHARLES FOSTER

doubleday

TRANSWORLD PUBLISHERS
Penguin Random House, One Embassy Gardens,
8 Viaduct Gardens, London SW11 7BW
www.penguin.co.uk

Transworld is part of the Penguin Random House group of companies
whose addresses can be found at global.penguinrandomhouse.com

First published in Great Britain in 2023 by Doubleday
an imprint of Transworld Publishers

A CIP catalogue record for this book
is available from the British Library.

ISBN 9780857529381

Typeset in 11.5/15pt Granjon LT Std by Jouve (UK), Milton Keynes.
Printed and bound in Great Britain by Clays Ltd, Elcograf S.p.A.

The authorized representative in the EEA is Penguin Random House Ireland,
Morrison Chambers, 32 Nassau Street, Dublin D02 YH68.

Penguin Random House is committed to a sustainable future
for our business, our readers and our planet. This book is made
from Forest Stewardship Council® certified paper.

For Jamie and Rachel, who help me keep faith with the wild, and for my mother and father, who have *gone* wild

In a business-as-usual scenario, the ocean is expected to contain 1 tonne of plastic for every 3 tonnes of fish by 2025, and by 2050, more plastics than fish (by weight).

World Economic Forum, *The new plastics economy: rethinking the future of plastics*, 2016

ἡ γὰρ ἀποκαραδοκία τῆς κτίσεως τὴν ἀποκάλυψιν τῶν υἱῶν τοῦ θεοῦ ἀπεκδέχεται...

οὐ μόνον δέ, ἀλλὰ καὶ αὐτοὶ τὴν ἀπαρχὴν τοῦ πνεύματος ἔχοντες ἡμεῖς καὶ αὐτοὶ ἐν ἑαυτοῖς στενάζομεν υἱοθεσίαν ἀπεκδεχόμενοι, τὴν ἀπολύτρωσιν τοῦ σώματος ἡμῶν...

For the creation waits with eager longing for the revealing of the children of God ... We know that the whole creation has been groaning together as it suffers together the pains of labour ...

Romans 8: 19 and 22 (New Revised Standard Version)

My heart is fixed firm and stable in the belief that ultimately the sunshine and the summer, the flowers and the azure sky, shall become, as it were, interwoven into man's existence. He shall take from all their beauty and enjoy their glory.

Richard Jefferies, *The Life of the Fields*

CONTENTS

Preface   xi

Fox   1
Orca   31
Human   59
Mayfly   73
Rabbit   91
Gannet   133
Otter   171
Eel   197

Epilogue   227
Author's note   229
Acknowledgements   233
Notes   235

PREFACE

I don't believe in climate change. Or mass extinction. Or the possibility that my children will grow up in a digitized desert ruled by sociopaths and robots. Not really. I can't. Those thoughts are too big and abstract to convince anything other than my brain. My brain is the least important part of me, and has little to do with my convictions, and so has little effect on what I actually *do*.

I'm a little, local person who sees himself as a story. And so I will be convinced only by little, local stories. I will worry myself sick about climate change if I can see it happening in a pond round the corner, and truncating or twisting the tale of an individual animal I care about. Particularly if the animal's plainly a fellow sufferer.

The natural world is under siege. Humans are banging at its gates and poisoning it and starving it. Its inhabitants are suffocating, diseased and neurotic. They're not the sort of creatures they're meant to be. Since we are all part of the natural world, I'm besieged too. Everything's a fellow sufferer – and particularly the arch-besiegers. Haven't you seen them on their way to the office?

We are used – indeed, over-used – to learning about the siege from the perspective of concerned humans. We're tired of the reportage: seals drowned in nets, seabirds strangled with those plastic rings from packs of beer, bone-dead coral, corned-beef factories where there was once rainforest, oiled gulls, thousand-acre fields of genetically modified maize. They're *too* dreadful for me. I should be horrified and ashamed, but instead I'm bored and in denial. And I can't relate at all to the figures detailing the catastrophe. Yes, they're bad. Yes, we're all going to die. Pass the salt, please. How's your homework, Rachel?

This exhaustion of our intellect, our compassion and our capacity for alarm is desperately dangerous. Only imagination can reignite them. And only story (whether written, painted, sung, danced or told round a fire) can do the necessary imaginative job. We're dying for want of a story. The stories commonly peddled today (the story of the free market, of atomistic entities of merely economic significance) have got us to where we are. We need to rip them up; to say that they're not good enough for creatures like us, or like rabbits, otters or gannets.

There's been lots of ripping. Great. It's a fine sound. But now there has to be some storytelling. New storytelling, which is always, if it's the real thing, the recapitulation of the old, old stories.

We need now to tell those new–old stories of the natural world from the perspective of the besieged. That's why I've written this book.

Some of these animals in this book are emotional in a way that humans can understand. That will raise some eyebrows. It shouldn't. It used to be disreputable to talk about animal emotion (though Darwin himself wrote a prescient and under-read book about animal emotion, published in 1871). But it is so no longer – though in the academy one has to choose one's words carefully, forcing them into the established pigeonholes of neo-Darwinian orthodoxy. Animal emotion is now a science. We know that animals feel, and something of what they are likely to be feeling. They are not automata. This science can and must inform our understanding of the moral significance of our eco-cidal psychopathy, and any literary attempt to understand what it is like to be one of the besieged. I'm with the American biologist Carl Safina on anthropomorphism: it lets you make a good first guess at what an animal is feeling. We shouldn't be satisfied with the first guess – there are always caveats to be inserted – but nor should we resign ourselves to thinking that we can't begin to think what an animal is feeling. That's very unscientific. Many non-human animals have more or less the same neurological hardware as we have – and, so far as we can tell, the same affective software. That software is used in the same contexts that we use ours. Otherness generally – human as well as non-human – is scarily inaccessible, but we can make some progress in getting outside our own heads, and it's urgently important to try.

I often wonder if those who remain sceptical about animal emotion have ever seen a dog who's been thoroughly thrashed. Or, even more convincingly, one who's been thoroughly loved. Dogs, I agree, are something of a special case, since they've co-evolved with us for so long that it's hard to know where the dog ends and its owner begins. But we see the same emotional colours if we look elsewhere in the animal world: at cetaceans, for instance.

I wonder, too (though I'd never argue the point) if our human ideas of epic and symphony mightn't be anaemic beside the corresponding ideas of non-humans whose sensors are more fully switched on than ours, and who recruit a wider range of sensory modalities than we do.

In these stories about individual animals I often talk about, or assume, the individual's *reason* for doing something. Often I do so with grave misgivings – mainly because much of what we conclude about animal motive is derived from studies of populations, and inferences from populations to individuals are (as we know from human examples) very dubious.

Take, for instance, our gannet's decision to fly south instead of east.

Let's imagine that we could demonstrate conclusively that the fishing grounds off the coast of Western Sahara were objectively better for gannets than those off the Algerian coast – and accordingly that to head south conferred an advantage that massively outweighed any extra costs of going that way.

Flying south would thus be advantageous to a *population*, and on balance and on average it would be better for an individual to belong to the southward group. The 'advantage' on which so much biological theorizing rests lurks in graphs, and gannets don't understand graphs. Graphs are abstractions, and gannets don't do abstractions of that kind. They have eyes for concrete things like the fatness of another gannet's body, but unless it can plausibly be said (and it can't) that the eastward gannets see that the southward gannets' bodies are better, or that there's an eloquent and effective bush telegraph (to which the Mediterranean birds are deaf) extolling the virtues of the West African fleshpots, the 'decision' of an individual bird to go to the capelin grounds off Ad Dakhla rather than the sandeel fishery off Tunis isn't the result of anything we'd call a *reason*.

There's another reason I'm uneasy about invoking reasons. It is that the 'reasons' we name and discuss as such inhabit the realm of the conscious. Yet surely almost nothing interesting or significant happens to us at the level of our consciousness. To call us Homo *sapiens* is a joke. Most of what 'I' am and what 'I' do wells up from far, far below the surface of the conscious 'me'. Why should we assume that it's any different for (for instance) birds – particularly when we're so keen to deny them any consciousness at all? Perhaps, like us, they're mostly subconscious or unconscious? Which doesn't make them, any more than it makes us, machines.

All that said, it is sometimes surely right to use the word 'reason' unapologetically in explaining animal behaviour. Does anyone reflective really doubt the foresight of animals? That dog that's been beaten by his master cringes when the master comes home, knowing that soon the stick will come down again on his back. A gull detaches from a feeding party and flies across the sea to an island because it has in its mind (yes, its *mind*!) a picture of something that exists in a time yet to come, a time that can only be imagined: a time of mussels or safety or sexual opportunity. It's that picture that drives the wings and sets the bird's face in unmistakable purposefulness. Acting in accordance with the picture – acting in the light of foresight – is a fairly classic instance of what we would call 'reasoned' behaviour.

Sometimes in these stories I indicate explicitly that some entities in the natural world other than individual organisms have *agency*. The sea, for instance, or a wave in the sea. This is not merely a literary device. In common with Upper Palaeolithic hunter-gatherers and the best and most swashbuckling quantum physicists, I take the view that consciousness is ubiquitous – an irreducible, fundamental part of the weave of the cosmos, which is somehow individuated by the shape and quality of the matter (whatever that is) to which it is related. My own experience of the natural world is of listening in on a conversation, and conversation entails agency.

Stories about animals have an ancient and patchy history.

Probably the very first stories told by humans around Palaeolithic camp fires involved animals, and probably among the very first exercises of the creative human faculty were attempts to probe otherness: to reconstruct the lives of non-humans, and to wonder what it is like to be a non-human. Animals were recruited by Aesop to make points about human conduct, and there is an unbroken line of heredity from Aesop to Beatrix Potter, George Orwell and Richard Adams.

At their best, fictional animal stories have an extraordinary capacity to engage imagination and change perspectives. Ted Hughes said that Henry Williamson's *Tarka the Otter* (1927) was the 'holy book' of his youth – the first thing to make him feel 'the pathos of actuality in the natural world'. Rachel Carson declared that *Tarka* and Williamson's book *Salar the Salmon* (1935) were two of the three books she would take to a desert island.

An academic commentator, writing about *Tarka*, observed that 'any careful reader of *Tarka* will readily perceive its much greater similarity to scientifically and philosophically interventionist works like Carson's [*Under the Sea Wind*] and [Barbara] Gowdy's [*The White Bone*] than to more overtly anthropomorphising works for children or young adults such as Kenneth Grahame's *The Wind in the Willows* and Richard Adams' *Watership Down*'. I agree.

Anthropomorphic tales have their place (and anthropomorphism as a *method of investigation* most certainly does) but they tend to perpetuate the toxic assumption that humans are the only fit subject for literature. It is Tarka-type stories that can and must do for modern readers what *Tarka* itself did for Ted Hughes.

I hope that's what these stories are.

Each story is free-standing. They can be read in any order.

Some of the stories contain violent images which some will find distressing or triggering. A good (or bad) example is the very start of the rabbit story, where there is an account of a rape of one rabbit by another. I've been urged to take that out, and though I'm truly sorry for any distress I've caused, I have resisted. If we're to tell the truth about humans it's only fair to tell the truth about rabbits too. But we need to be careful about what the 'truth' here is. Of course we shouldn't judge human conduct by reference to the actions or inactions of non-humans. There's no moral equivalence between the rape of a rabbit by a rabbit and the rape of a human by a human. One other point: The human anti-hero of the rabbit story was conceived in circumstances similar to the rabbit. It should go without saying that those circumstances neither explain nor excuse the way he chose to live.

I often refer to 'our rabbit', 'our otter' and so on. I've done it because it's convenient, but I'm uneasy about it. No wild thing is *ours*, except in the vital sense that everything is everybody's and everything is everyone's responsibility. A companionable sense (which makes me, for instance, talk proudly and inaccurately about 'my swifts' – the ones that nest in the eaves just above my head in my study in Oxford) can mutate easily into a sense of entitled proprietorship. And just look where that's got us.

The species in this book are chosen to illustrate the types of weapons we humans use in our war on the wild.

I hate polemic, but find that I've written a very polemical book. But really, what choice did I have?

FOX

Vulpes vulpes

He was born under a corporate lawyer's shed, a hundred yards from one of the main arteries pumping people and things into London. The clay of his birth-den throbbed. Next to the road was a railway which shook worms on to his head during the morning and evening rush hours.

The fox cub's first bone was from this clay. It was about fifty million years old, and came from the wing of an Eocene proto-sparrow which had picked tropical horseflies from palm trees in Bethnal Green.

The cub's second bone came from the wing of a feral pigeon that had been hit by a van delivering pork pies.

That second bone came when he was eight weeks old, for until then his parents, committed, sophisticated and cynical urbanites, had brought him mainly pizza (they preferred pepperoni), and curry (with a bias towards chicken tikka masala) from the bounteous dustbins of the East End.

The lawyer's older children didn't know and wouldn't have cared that they had wild things in their garden: things more cat than dog, with rotatable ears and pupils that could change their shape depending on the intensity of the light; things that inhabited that grid of terraced streets far more intensely and intimately than the humans who'd mortgaged themselves to it and slaved to stay there. Those older children didn't really live in the street at all. They fuelled up in an actual world so that they could live in a virtual one. They have no part in this story.

But the lawyer had a young child. To her siblings she was a bore and an irritation.

Like many young children who can walk on two legs, she much preferred to walk on four, for then her nose was nearer the ground, and her palms soaked up sensation rather than hanging wastefully loose. Like the head of an agile flower she followed the sun. She acknowledged no boundary between herself and any non-humans, and no continuity with her siblings – for whom her contempt was complete.

She saw the fox cub the very first time he put his nose out of the ground, for she was lying on the trouble-free plastic grass watching earwigs. Eyes rarely meet without any preconceptions, but they did then, and when that happens the melding of worlds is potently alchemical. New stuff is created; stuff impossible according to the canons of chemistry or biology. The new stuff became part of the matrix of each and every cell in both bodies. If the matrix dissolved, the cells would collapse.

She did not give the fox cub a name. She had heard her parents call her by her name, and heard in it the claim of possession and control. This fox was self-possessed and self-controlled, and she knew that to control him would be to kill him. He was also, like the rest of the wild world, part of her, and since she did not accept that she could be named, she paid the fox the compliment of namelessness. All names, she knew, fall short.

And so I will not name her either.

The fox cub was her secret. She would no more have thought of telling her despairing childminder or her occasional parents about him than she would have thought of asking her brother for a look at his Instagram account.

She did not seek *information* about the fox cub – let alone information about foxes. The girl wanted only presence. All her five senses – and many, many more – were involved in the appreciation of presence, but they all worked together in a sort of multimodal palpation. This was palpation *by* as well as *of* the fox cub. Until we're five, reciprocity rules. After that we learn to be alone.

The girl had not learned to be alone, and would have been disgusted to hear that it was expected of her. She was a wild thing in a wild place. No Metropolitan Borough Council told the beetles where to march or the sparrows where to fly, or decided when the magpies died. Though she lived in a house of deadly cleanliness, where every surface was swabbed with chemicals to keep wildness at bay, the air, even in the immaculately white living room, was full of spores erupting on cheese, plaster or skin, and viruses waiting to inject their RNA into house flies or au pairs; and the gut of the girl's father, filled though it was with oysters and white burgundy from business lunches, was a bubbling vat of bacteria without which he'd be dead. The electric currents in the mother's heart had gone wild the previous year, which had caused a bit of a panic in the Tuscan hills, and there was a sporting chance, according to the actuaries, that both the mother and the father would finally fall because the cells in her breast and his prostate would decide, wildly and disloyally, to go walkabout as their owners never had. And when the father and mother fell, they would go completely wild through a municipal chimney.

The girl, then, was wise to live as she, a wild thing, really was, in the place (wild, gentrified Bethnal Green) where she really was. Such a kind of living is almost unknown for modern adults, and an adult who lives that way is quite likely to be locked up in a secure unit where they'll meet a rather different kind of wildness, as well as the old sort.

The fox cub, despite the pressures of urban life, was never likely to stop being wild, which meant that he was never likely to stop being himself.

Being oneself involves having preferences. He did. He preferred the top left nipple, his sister with the extra claw, dawn to dusk, the smell of petrol to the smell of diesel, rats to squirrels for play – though not for eating – roses to chrysanthemums, Labradors to Jack Russells, almost anything to cats, chow mein to spring rolls, rump steak to fillet and lamb to pork, Costcutter to Tesco, mango to kiwi, women to men, oaks to sycamores, tangledness to tidiness, chicken legs to breasts, voles to shrews, human harmony to human conflict (he got a good view of the family arguments from a bed of azaleas), and worms to black beetles.

These preferences were strong. He was an opinionated, headstrong fox cub, about to become an opinionated headstrong fox. His mother almost despaired of him, and would have despaired of him if natural selection had let her.

He spent one exhilarating day in a central reservation, crouched inside a lorry tyre, his hair standing on end, deafened, shaken like a cocktail, and inhaling a cocktail of rubber, lead, cadmium, and many compounds from the bodies of Carboniferous sea animals from Arabia.

He ran so fast after a squirrel that his momentum carried him halfway up a yew tree where he was marooned for a day and saw, as few foxes ever get to see, just how human hair springs from the scalp, and how it sometimes gives up growing completely.

He learned how to read the swinging of the iron particles in his own body which told him not in which direction a vole was (triangulation of the squeaks that came to his swivelling ears told him that), but how far away it was, and learned to leap high like a cat so that he could have the vole on visual for the last few milliseconds of the approach. He learned, too, that all this sophisticated hardware and software did not disclose a nest of used hypodermic needles, and that when his nose bristled with needles it was hard to grab them with his paws and pull them out, and that if he rubbed his nose on the ground they never came out but produced abscesses that hardened into lumps which made him lopsided for ever.

He learned that prawn sandwiches were dumped outside the corner shop at eight o'clock, but also that the gate was locked at nine, and that the gate and the wall were harder to climb than yew trees, and that when he ran between the legs of the woman who opened the gate in the morning she screeched almost in ultrasound, which he hadn't thought humans could do.

He learned that bats could sometimes be caught as he caught flies, but that they tasted of leather soaked in the piss of police horses and had teeth that hooked into his gums.

He discovered that people like cats, and that if you chased one, or even ate a dead one at the roadside, windows eased slyly up and there'd be a crack thwack sting and then a little metal nodule under your skin.

Though he was young for it, he discovered grief too, though not in the acute form he met later. His siblings were dead before their first birthday.

One stood bemused by the headlights of a speeding car, and the car hit it as our fox watched from the kerb, and it burst; but the worst of it was that it lay there for a week, flattened and mangled, and deep inside our fox that didn't seem right – and not just because mourning at the place where the body lay was difficult and dangerous: it was a matter of some old stern propriety: some choreographic rule had been violated, and the dance of the whole world was spoiled.

Half of London's foxes die in road traffic accidents, but that road traffic accident made our anarchic little fox prefer old, slow, rustic ways, and distrust motors.

Another sister ate rat poison, and though the unclotting blood leaked from her mouth and into her eyes, it was the bleeding inside that made her double up and moan. Right at the end she found the convulsive strength to kick our fox in the face as her back legs cycled – and then she was gone, the fox didn't know where, leaving a body that looked and smelt like her for a day, and then changed. Our fox knew that something that had been present had left, which I suppose makes him a kind of philosopher.

And the third, having woven artfully around the traffic and sniffed every bit of food suspiciously, stopped eating and slept too much and then her hair started to fall out and she shrank until she looked like a toast rack and her eyes were the biggest bits of her. One day, as the human parents barked directions to the children and bolted to the office, she slipped away to join – our fox mistily supposed – the other dead cubs.

The fox cub had never played much with the other cubs. He was too interested in the non-foxy world. But now, alone with his mother (who was already thinking about her next litter), he wondered what he had missed.

There was still the girl. Her attentions were more intense than ever. As soon as she'd been put to bed she got up again, flung open the bedroom window, propped her head on her hands and watched. She admired the untimetabled life of the fox. Her days were carefully scripted, though she tore up and befouled the script whenever she could. But the fox, if it pleased him, rose with the moon and, if it pleased him, sank into the earth as the moon rose from it. If he wanted to eat, he ate, and if he wanted to be leaner and alert, he didn't. There was no need to hunt, for the streets oozed calories, but often he chose to do so in obedience to an old and insistent voice that sometimes the girl thought she could hear too. Sometimes, too, to the horror of her carers, she obeyed the voice herself, lying in wait for the park squirrels with a bag of throwable stones under the park rhododendrons, knocking pigeons off the bird table with a catapult made according to the instructions in the *Boys' Own Paper*, *c.* 1924, which she'd found mouldering in the attic, and wearing at night, when she knew she wouldn't be disturbed, a cap made from the skin of a rabbit covertly gathered and skinned on the family holiday in Tuscany.

She saw the fox on most days, and was glad when she did. He looked always up to her window and pulled back his lips in what she told herself was a smile. But sometimes she did not see him, and was gladder still, for that meant he was still wild and unpredictable and not controlled by her or by habit, and still less by her bloody mother.

They grew up together.

They did not frolic. There was no shaking of paws or rough and tumble in the rockery; but, instead, the far more potent electricity of a quadrille, where palms barely touch and hips never; where the dancers circle, gaze and bow. He was the main tutor, yet she taught him, too. He taught her the solemn patterns of the dance he had learned when his brother died, and the wild mandate: dance on, even when the dance seems disrupted, for the pattern can always be restored. He taught her the importance of being claimed by a place, even if the place has AstroTurf over the bones of the dinosaurs and the strongest mobile phone signal in the Western world. He affirmed what she knew already: that all is wild, and that we're best off if we live as if it is.

And she taught him that an abiding presence is precious.

She learned that the only lasting things are relationships, and that since everything is relationship, everything lasts – which is a terrible and glorious thought. I cannot believe that she taught him this: there is too much syntax involved. But he felt the power that streams from that belief, and it was that power that drew his eyes to the bedroom window.

They all thought she was odd, and her pride and humility were such that she didn't care. Her parents, when they were told by her school to notice her, sent her to a well-meaning woman who ran a battery of tests and asked lots of questions, and the girl obediently did the tests and smiled at the questions and gave the answers she knew were expected, and the well-meaning woman wrote a long report saying that so far as she could see the girl was within the normal distribution, that there was no evidence of organic disease, that no focused psychiatric intervention could responsibly be prescribed, but that nonetheless she retained an intangible sense of unease. She thought that this last phrase would keep her insurers happy. She concluded that time and conventional schooling would probably lay to rest any fears the parents might have.

The girl started to keep a diary. It included details of the weather, and particularly where she thought the weather had come from – for that gave her a sense of the size and connectedness of the world, and she loved to think of Honduran spiders being dumped by the rain on to the dahlias. It included too the activities of the ants, the appearances and diet of the garden birds, sketches of her anatomical dissections (mostly small mammals and birds brought in by the cat), and searingly honest assessments of her own developing prowess as a taxidermist. But mostly it was about the fox: time of appearance, apparent mood, state of the coat, condition score (which she'd discovered in a book on sheep farming). And, more than anything else, the fox's diet. For he often showed her what he'd brought home to the ancestral home under the shed, waggling it in his mouth as he looked up to the window, and putting it down on the ground so that she could get a better view if she seemed doubtful. She'd look at his dung, too, mixing it up with water in a jam jar and pouring the mixture through muslin to display the undigested bits.

One night she noticed that he was abandoning the dustbins. He wasn't eating much pizza or Sunday roast. Instead his scat was flecked with the tiny bones of rodents and small birds – the hardest things of all for a fox to catch. She saw, too, tension in his gait. He no longer flowed through the streets, but stamped. In a human toddler it would have been resentment.

There was change enough in her own life, and she didn't like this change in the fox at all. She took to following him at a long and respectful distance. If he changed direction, he always waited for her to catch up. He went every night to the railway line. At first she thought it was the hunting, for no strimmer or spray had touched the side of the embankment, and small mammals lived unmolested, except by fox, weasel and kestrel, in the catacombs they had pushed through the thick grass.

But he did not come here for the food. There were bodies enough in the gardens and the loading yards behind the shops.

He came, it seemed, to stare and to sniff. He sat alert on his haunches on a couch of rosebay willow herb which gave him a long view up and down the line.

He paid particular attention when a train clanked past. It looked to the girl as if he stiffened. His nose rose and tightened, and often, when the train had gone, he got off his couch and trotted down to the line and walked with his nose down along the rails. And then he sloped back to the couch and looked long and only in the direction from which incoming trains came and to which outgoing trains were going. Never, ever, towards town.

Then he started to go missing. The diaries record the absences. She had always marked with a red cross the nights when he didn't appear. Now there were long, unbroken sequences of crosses. Then he would reappear, lay a trophy down for her to see as of old, and she would tell herself that all was well again. But at last the crosses couldn't be denied.

The railway line threaded through slashes in the London clay, past banks of houses that once held huge families of dockers, cabbies and sweatshop slaves and now held brokers with kitchens fitted round them, out through remnants of woodland pocked with fake Tudor mansions with entryphones and automatic garage doors, through embattled farmland with profit margins so tight the farmers hadn't breathed for a generation, and finally to the heaving sea, still heavy with the filth of the capital.

Sometimes the farmers stopped breathing altogether, and their farms passed to people so rich that the land could retire from farming, too. When it did, the land declared its true colours within the year. When it was allowed to rot, life sprang from the corpses. The land had never stopped waiting. It had only ever been in exile – and exile right there, under the noses of the agricultural economists, waiting to confound, outrage, rebuild and re-enchant.

The re-enchantment was literal. There was birdsong again once the clearing and the poisoning stopped, and with the birdsong came the rushes of sparrowhawks between the branches, their yellow legs outstretched to grip, and the high whistle of air past the folded wings of stooping peregrines. Voles, shrews and long-tailed field mice fought, fed and bred under the new tangle. Kestrels, watching for them, hovered and fell, hovered and fell, until their shift was taken over by barn owls, ghosting through the last of the light.

The farmers had waged a fitful, inconclusive war against the rabbits in the hedge bottoms and the copses, and though the rich men's sons sometimes wandered the hedges with a gun and a fat spaniel, and there were sometimes dirt cheap rabbits to be had behind the pub, the rabbits were soon grazing insolently everywhere. Foxes came from the city to graze on them.

I don't know if our fox, when he sniffed the railway line, was sniffing these new colonizing foxes. They did sometimes go to the railway line, and when they did, no doubt wanted to stake their claim to such a dramatic feature (much more obvious and desirable than their usual marking spots of tussocks and the summits of gentle rises) by defecating and urinating on the line. But I do like to think that our fox was getting messages, perhaps through his nose, or perhaps through one of the many other stranger and more potent senses we all have, about another way of being a fox; another way of doing life; a way bracingly and companionably concordant with those long engrained preferences of his – preferences which looked in the inner city like perversities.

Whatever the reason, he started to walk at night along the railway line, always east, and always walking, never foraging or hunting. Each night he went further than the night before, and each night the sense of another way of existing grew stronger.

He met other foxes walking along the line. They were focused, rather brassy commuters. Some earned their living in the city and came back to the fresher air of Essex to play and to sleep, with their bellies full of metropolitan trash. And some earned their living in the country, eating real food honestly won, and then, for some reason, trotted back into the city to digest their rabbit and pheasant as they snoozed under the decking in a gentrified Edwardian terrace. Though he met the commuters, our fox had no way of interrogating them about what they were doing. Foxes don't work like that. But he saw their movements, and knew the wild on them and sometimes in them, and it made him restless. They injected new possibilities.

We must be clear. Foxes are concrete thinkers. They have little taste and less aptitude for abstraction. But some things that we tend to think of as abstractions are irresistibly alluring to the concrete brains of foxes: freedom (and not just because it means you have a chance of killing more things); wild (and not just because it means that you're not boxed in by streets and patios); silence (and not just because the rustlings of mice are more audible). The attraction of such things to the normally disposed fox could not be justified by the imperatives of survival or reproduction. It is far closer to what, in humans, is often mocked as passionate romanticism than it is to anything else. So there it is: our fox is a Romantic, squarely in the tradition of Wordsworth, Coleridge and Ruskin. The girl never doubted it. It was this that made her able to bear his increasing absenteeism, and eventually his absence. If he had abandoned her on a poetical quest it wasn't quite so hurtful.

She had long known that he wasn't hers. Like all proper loves, her love had nothing to do with possession, and would be defeated by possession. The fox was *other*, and decent people only ever love the *other*. He didn't look, walk, smell, think or urinate like her. The world through which he stalked was immeasurably, unimaginably different from hers, though according to the four dreary dimensions in which sober humans think in the daytime, they occupied the same tidy garden somewhere along the Central Line.

If he was not hers, whose was he? He was self-possessed, to be sure (and self-possession is so rare among humans that it's very obvious whenever it's there, whether in humans or foxes). But he was also part of the scintillating matrix of relationships which she now knew was called *wild*: and wildness was that quadrille: *was* the relationship she had with him. She'd already learned a few steps, and knew the modes in which the music was played. Unlike human music, its cadences could be both major and minor, or neither, for the wild writes the rules and can dissolve them if it chooses, as it often does.

He'd danced away along the railway line, perfectly in time to the music.

I've told of the electricity between the fox and the girl: those long looks from and to the bedroom window. The relationship between them wasn't just in her head. It was in his head and his body too. He couldn't imagine having a head or a body in which she wasn't present. How then could he just waltz off to rural Essex, leaving her pining? Doesn't that give the lie to all the grand protestations about their mutual entanglement?

It certainly would, if that were all there was to say about it.

But it never, ever occurred to the fox that the girl wouldn't or couldn't follow. Foxes are simple things. This is how he thought: she looked out of the window and followed me along the street because she, unlike the rest of the two-legged ones, is wild. I am going to the wild. That must be where she is from. Things go back to where they are from. She will come to the wild, too, and there we will know one another properly.

But it wasn't so easy. A twelve-year-old (as she now was) can't get a train to the middle of nowhere – even if nowhere is where the wild is, and she's always *really* lived in the wild – and wander through farmland shouting the name of a fox who she has always known has no name at all.

The fox moved into his country house one bitter January night. He looked up to the window, but the girl was out, learning, despite her best efforts, to be a good citizen. He took one last glance at laughing people giving away money on TV, and set off east along the line at a slow, sustainable lope.

He knew where he was going. He had found it several months before – an old badger sett in a steep bank in a clump of snoring sycamores, looking down on a field which was a natural proving ground for humans, and had been the site of several forgotten battles. On his first night there the fox ate a family of field mice born in the skull of a Danish Viking who had looked the wrong way at a crucial moment. A Roman femur was the main joist of his sleeping chamber.

The badgers – weakened by psychopaths in camouflage trousers who had dragged them out with long iron tongs, tied them in sacks, broken their teeth and sometimes a leg and then set dogs on them – had finally been cleared out by the local dairy farmer, who, blaming them rather than a cut-price heifer for the TB in his herd, gassed them and let them rot. The fox pulled out what he could of their carcasses, and trampled the rest into the earth.

There was no shortage of food, but the fox had to range widely for it. Rabbits took some hunting. They didn't just freeze and wait for him to pounce, as his urban voles had done. He had to watch where he placed his soft cat's feet; had to learn to curve his body as he crept forward for the kill, so that it didn't snag on thorns. He had to learn about wind; not just to keep the rabbits upwind, but to know how the wind would behave in the hollows; how it would eddy and where it would spin away; which trees made it rebound and which trees stopped and absorbed it. The city had been olfactorily deafening. He could use his nose there for very crude investigation: how old a pork pie was, how dead a cat was, how deeply a guinea-pig was buried. But there was too much noise in his nose for fine distinctions. He didn't need to make them, anyway. You only lived there, it seemed to him now, if you wanted to avoid nuance.

He was a late starter, but an astute and diligent learner. He applied himself to the art and science of the moving air and the shifting seasons. He had no tutors. He sometimes saw other foxes out and about. Most were related to one another, and looked sceptically at our fox from a distance, sometimes running at him with bared teeth. But a childhood of pizza makes a bigger body than a childhood of spindly rabbit. He stood his ground because he did not understand the language of aggression. This was taken as strength, and soon he was left alone.

Being alone started to bother him. Or, rather, posterity started to taunt him. Chemically normal though he was, when he was in the city he'd sublimated his lust into his regime of hunting and wandering. But the city was never his place, and as some humans defer reproduction until they have a house and an income deemed fit for offspring, and some animals delay implantation until the time is right, so he had deferred impregnation.

But he was now four. That made him old. Few London foxes reach such an advanced age. He was finally in his place, and there were perils all around, and if there ever was to be a time, it was now.

Soon after he arrived a vixen screamed her availability to the moon. She was a long way off, in a beech stockade on the crest of a long ridge. The fox had scouted the place before, catching a hen pheasant whose wing had been mashed by a poor shot on a corporate bonding day. He had smelt her then on a pile of wet leaves, though she was not there, and he had trembled. Now he galloped, squeezing through gates and over the barbed wire and under the electric fences which carved up the land. Cattle parted before him, sheep scattered, and low-roosting wood pigeons clattered and scrambled further up their trees. He ignored in his urgency a moaning rabbit being strangled by a wire snare, a cowering chicken that hadn't been locked up for the night, and the pungent afterbirth of a lamb.

He knew somehow what he would find: the vixen in the middle of a glade, dog foxes around her. She would be coy, slow and picky. She knew it was a seller's market. The stakes were high and Darwin was the market-maker. She couldn't afford to waste an expensive pregnancy; to invest in something with a sub-optimal return. She would choose on the basis of aggression, size and persistence, for those are the crude metrics of value in the fox's world. Before she submitted, teeth had to be sharp, reflexes brisk, endurance endless, desire ablaze.

There were five dog foxes when he arrived, all of them

brothers or cousins, all in a smouldering standoff that sometimes flared. Then snarling balls of fur rolled down the hill, ears were ripped and noses punctured, and sometimes teeth met in a neck and then one of the foxes slunk off into the dark with its head down.

Our fox had timed it well. The fighting had been going on for a while. The survivors were tired and the vixen aroused. But the dog foxes were not ready to let their efforts go to waste, and their natural desperation was fuelled by xenophobia. So, for the first time in his life, our fox was up against something that badly wanted to hurt him. This encounter with concentrated intention was a shock. He had known intention in himself – when he had hunted – but it did not have this quality or intensity. This intention was hot and red, beyond personality and immune to appeal. Teeth closed with the force that comes from the geological weight of aeons. The malevolence was the distilled struggle and angst of Cambrian fossils.

But there is only so much that primordial hate can do against pepperoni pizza, and soon, mud- and blood-stained, and with a punctured pad, he took the vixen there, under a beech tree, and limped back with her to the badger sett, where, for the next two days, they copulated until he was spent and changed and the loneliness had drained away.

He was an intermittent husband, but a diligent father of the four cubs pushed out by the vixen in April, as the first swallows returned and the first hawthorn flowers frothed over the hedges. He did more than a dog fox's usual share of the hunting, and much more of the playing and schooling.

He had left fatherhood late, and didn't want to miss out now; but he knew, too, that he needed the cubs to teach him the lessons about being a proper fox that his urban youth and eccentric proclivities had denied him. He watched them; not crowding, not proscribing anything other than immediate danger; not prescribing at all. He tried to keep pace with their tiny feet, the thrumming of their hearts and the working of their jaws. He noted their instinctual tastes and tried to share them. He lay flat, seeing at their eye and nose level the mice and moles he brought for their killing classes, the aphids tapping the columns of rising sap, the glistening slime-roads of snails, the lice in birds' armpits, the glass cutlass edges of grass, the hairy metal legs of ladybirds, the blackberry eyes of flies, the hooks that stop feathers unzipping. He listened with them to the stories told by what he had once thought was silence; the flutter of a stoat's heart, the check in a woodcock's throat as it decides not to cry, the different accents of oak depending on whether the wind came from east or west, the thump of nuts dropped by a careless squirrel, the scratch-squeak-click of shrew claws in sand.

More importantly he sat obediently at their feet as, with brains unconstricted by presumption, with no valves regulating the flow of data from the vast universe outside, they discovered and practised ways of knowing that had little to do with sensation. They knew where their mother was, though sight, smell, sound and knowledge of her habits gave no clue. They knew what a rabbit would do, though the rabbit did not know itself. Silent clouds boomed. They became highly competent naturalists, recognizing hundreds of species. And they became highly competent supernaturalists, as we tragic truncated humans have to say – we having surrendered, for nothing in return, dozens of natural senses. And we wonder why we don't feel at home in the world.

The cubs helped him to shake off the city because the city

was the place of not-noticing and not-knowing, and they helped him to notice and to know. By the time they were weaned, he too was weaned from the city.

Foxes are often basically monogamous, with lapses. Our fox had no lapses. His vixen was quite enough. That, perhaps, was because of his crash course in noticing. He knew that the more he looked – whether at a pheasant's egg, the tantalizing door of a henhouse, the ghost of a long-dead farm labourer, or at the vixen, the more there was to see.

He fed the vixen while she was closeted with the suckling cubs, as most fox fathers do; but after that, when others tended to detach themselves from the family, move away from the natal burrow and live out in the open, he stayed at the badger sett, his family round him, continuing the programme of learning in the strenuous school of relationship and attention.

The land had given him what he needed and wanted, and in this bursting spring it continued to give – by taking from others. He and the family grew sleek on young rabbits, nests of blind pink mice, eggs and nestlings, and on young birds who didn't make it into the air on the first attempt. He could not help noticing that the cries of the mothers were like the cries he had made when he saw his own brother dead on the London road, but I do not know what he did with that noticing.

Most foxes are catholic eaters – omnivores with a very varied diet – and having been brought up in London he was more catholic than most, and raised his children that way. He had a taste for earthworms, scratching for them in damp earth and eating them untidily as we'd eat tagliatelle without a fork; and for the big black slugs that look to humans as if they should taste of liquorice, and for roots and bulbs to clean his teeth, in which he had an unseemly pride. He had, too, a fastidious dislike of carrion, but he did not transmit this to the cubs, who thought decomposition piquant, as human children like barbecue sauce.

One spring day his fussiness saved him. A very late lamb, the result of a desperate, underused tup pushing through a hedge and finding a rare ewe that had not been served with the main batch, had been born outside, no one realizing the mother was pregnant. The naïve mother abandoned it, it died of pneumonia, and its corpse was pulled around by foxes, who left footprints, red hairs and tell-tale scat.

The farmer found the corpse and tried and convicted the foxes in their absence. He sentenced them to death, choosing strychnine, which he kept illegally for poisoning moles.

The fox family found the baited body that evening. Our fox, who wouldn't have found the stinking lamb tempting at the best of times, circled it, smelling the sour stink of men and something else, and yapped at the cubs to stay away.

Two disobeyed, tugging at the guts. In such small bodies the effect was almost immediate. It started with a grimace, and then everything stiffened and shivered, and the shivering made heat so great that their brains began to harden like boiled eggs, and then, because the muscles on the top of their backs and necks were stronger than the muscles that opposed them, their necks and backs bent back as if they needed to touch their tails with their ears, and so one cub cracked her own spine, but the other boiled herself dead before that could happen. Then our fox heard from himself, from places in himself which he had not known, the same cry, though in a different accent, as he had caused in others a thousand times that spring.

The farmer left the cubs to rot by the lamb, on the grounds

that it would teach foxes about revenge, and every night for a month, when the zoological journals say that he should have been hunting to maximize the chance of the survivors living to reproductive age, and to improve his own condition and sperm quality, he stayed by the bodies for hours, often silent, but sometimes raising his head to the moon and whining in a tone not used for anything else in his life, and sometimes lying with his head alongside each of the cubs, looking, it seemed, into eyes that had long been taken by the crows.

Often the vixen joined him in the vigil, and then they sat or lay side by side. No sound passed between them. Their complaints were not at one another, and the pain was magnified for being shared, and anyway there was nothing to *say* in any language, whether yapped or barked or framed in one of the dialects of foxy telepathy. The cubs were bone of her bone: calcium had drained from her into them. Her heart had beat for them. And yet, when the month was up, it was she who moved off to a distant spinney, leaving her mate, who lay still on the grass where the cubs had died.

The summer spread new and untried wings, sobbed, hooted, howled and galloped. But every leaf and every splitting chrysalis and each proboscis waving for the first time taunted the fox with their newness. Nothing would be properly new again, because there had been proper newness in the spring and then the newness twitched and moaned and went back into the earth.

He had rejoiced in the power of his legs and the feel of his tongue as it swung between his teeth when he was hot and running, and rejoiced, too, in the problem of choosing in every moment which one of the infinite possibilities to select. But it seemed now to him that the possibilities were few and stark: he could decide to live or not to live. If he decided to live, his legs, his teeth and his tongue would help him, but that was just them doing their job; it wouldn't make things right.

There were two other cubs, of course. I would like to say that his duty to them saved him and turned the movements of his legs back into joy. But it was not so. If the duty had been more onerous it might have been different, but they now needed little help from him, and wanted less.

Though they had never known winter, the cubs felt its approach in the slow retreat of the land gathering into itself; a shell hardening; a leaf making a fist; a tree setting its jaw. They knew that they had to prepare, along with everything else. There was winter in them too, they found, which worked through them as the days shortened, preparing them for itself.

Our fox's legs worked joylessly. His food was just fuel, the land just a plate. His vixen saw the dullness of his eyes and resolved to seek another mate when her ovaries next started to swell.

~

The silage was all cut. The bodies of the little things that had refused to run from their homes were rolled up with the grass into tight plastic bags. In the winter, cows sometimes got a taste of musty vinaigrette as they bit into a fermented shrew. Most farmers hereabouts had long since given up hay-making. Good hay was better than bad silage, they were fond of saying, but bad silage was better than bad hay, and to have good hay you had to have the gods on your side, and these days the account-ants never seemed to be at all confident that the gods could be propitiated. Good farming was about the elimination of contingency, wasn't it? Why invite judgement by pinning your hopes on a fortnight of sun? So the summer sunlight was shrink-wrapped and nibbled by bacteria until it smelt of sauerkraut, and only the under-achieving cows of a bent, tweedy, poor farmer smelt the summer in February.

The cutting of the grass seemed to hasten the withdrawal of the sun. It was as if the sun had been there for the grass, and now that the grass was down, there was no reason for the sun to stay. So away south the sun went, dragging with it the swallows and the martins and the little anonymous brown birds from the canopies. And the fox, who this summer had not noticed, as he once would have done, the swish of the swallows as they surfed over the meadow, brushing the seed-heads with their wingtips, noticed now the absence of the swish, and the winter, deep inside him since the death of the cubs, strengthened its grip.

The corn was cut now too, and birds and slow rabbits with it. Without the softening corn, the land was shown for what it was. Bowls and humps appeared, and the bowls, as if embarrassed, covered themselves with curling brown leaves from the shrinking woods, and the fox sat on the humps at night and looked out over the new cold fields.

One bright September morning, after a night made easy by an unlocked henhouse, the fox was woken in his bracken bed by the long scraping cry of a jay. He had lost many a kill to this raucous busybody bird, but the jay was on the other side of the wood, and certainly hadn't seen him now. He raised his head, scanned with his ears, and pulled the cold air into his nose, sifting it for anything unusual. There was nothing out of the ordinary to smell, but a brisk wind was blowing from him to the wood. There was a sound: a far-off thudding and jingling. He held his breath so that he could hear better, and so that tell-tale plumes of cloud didn't billow out of the bracken. The sounds got nearer, but they meant nothing to him. Then a rogue eddy of wind escaped from the main front. It hit him in the face: Horses. Humans. Dogs. The sort of dogs who live together and sleep in a heap. Different dogs: not the inert things that shambled sometimes along the paths, not knowing that he was watching them from a few feet away through a screen of sedge.

He got up, shook himself and walked uphill to a favoured spot where he could see the whole of the plain below the wood. A mounted procession was coming slowly towards the wood; perhaps twenty horses, their riders dressed mostly in tweed jackets rather than the grander black of the season proper, for this was the pre-season cub-hunting – a time for the youngest hounds to learn the ropes, to match the scent of real foxes in the wood with the scent that their instinct and breed-ing gave them every night in their dreams. At the head of the cavalcade was a dour, spare, weather-beaten man in a red coat. He was the professional huntsman. Behind him, squeezed into a coat of great vulgarity and perched on a shiny chestnut too good for ground like this, was the new Master, happier at the helm of her property development company than holding the reins of a lively horse.

The huntsman had something to prove that day. The Mas-ter, whom he roundly but silently despised, had had the effrontery to criticize some of the decisions he had made about hound breeding. Her! Question him, a fifth-generation fox-hunter, with a mantelpiece full of daily polished trophies from the Peterborough Hound Show! She – who'd been brought up in a Southend semi and had bought her Mastership, as she'd bought those too-tight breeches, with her slippery vulgar cleverness.

He'd show her. Rafter, now. Rafter, only nine months old, with a leech's bloodthirst yet steady as the huntsman's own seat on a galloping horse, had the paws of a bear and the nose of her great-great-grandmother who could follow a fox through a dense crowd at a sheep sale, and once did. Or so it seemed from the early indications out on exercise. This was her first proper outing. But Rafter wouldn't let him down. He'd never been so sure of anything.

And now, as he rode over the stubble to the lower edge of the wood, he saw Rafter with her nose down, watching her mother, Rachel, through the corner of her eye, and the pair pushing to the front of the pack.

An obedient distance behind the huntsman rode the mounted followers, and as the huntsman urged his hounds into the wood with a wave and a 'Goo on, me lovelies. Go wind him, Go find him', the field split into two, each section peeling off to one side of the wood after the two red-coated whippers-in. They surrounded the wood, their horses twenty yards from one another, slapping their boots with their whip handles to discourage foxes from breaking out into the open. The young hounds had to learn how to work the deep cover, and the young foxes had to be thinned out to reduce chaos later in the season, when the serious hunting started.

Slap, slap, slap went the whips on the boots. Rafter and Rachel, first over the fence and into the wood, whimpered as the first fox scent thrilled through them. Their tails ('sterns' to fox-hunters) swung ('feathered') like masts in a dinghy gale. They were picking up the drag the cubs had left in the night.

But the night was not long gone, and they did not have a long line to puzzle out before they would find where the cubs had laid up as the sun rose.

'Go wind him, go find him. Yai, yai, yai, yai, yaiiiiiiii,' cheered the huntsman, feeling his hounds' excitement in his nose and bowels. And they did. But the cubs had been taught to flatten themselves on the ground and breathe so gently, even when terrified, that their whiskers, buried deep in a nerve net, never felt the breath. And so Rafter and Rachel were almost on top of them before the cubs realized that the old strategy wasn't working, and that something new had to be done. They bolted together towards the old badger sett, but black and tan Bellman, arthritic but clairvoyant, got between them. They split up, hoping to rejoin by a fallen sycamore, but Dignity, Raven and Ariadne barred the way, baying, bounding and slavering. The cubs were never going to reach the sett. They turned back, flittered round Rafter and Rachel, who were closing in, and were off to the fence. There was a deeper sett in the bottom of a blackthorn hedge across the field: deep, old and twisting. If they could get there no terrier in the world would get them out.

Up to the fence. Just a hundred yards of easy ground to go. But when they got to the fence there was a 'slap, slap, slap', and the jingle of harness which is like hot needles stuck down fox ears, and the stench of humans, far worse than the scent of hounds, for the scent of hounds is just the scent of individual fox deaths, but the stench of humans is the scent of death to everything.

They could easily have broken through the picket. They could have run between the horses or through the horses' legs, and the slapping was just crass, not deadly. But they turned back into the wood.

~

The girl had come to her aunt's house by train the previous night, dropped off by her au pair.

'It'll do you good to be in the country,' her mother had said between emails. 'Get you out of yourself, and get you on to a pony. Your aunt's going to put you on Snowdrop. He'll see you right. Safe as houses. Early morning, though. It'll be fabulous. Wish I could join you. Have fun. See you Sunday. Ciao.'

~

From the *Eastern Horn and Hound*:

The Mytton Hunt had its first day's cub-hunting on Saturday. The meet was at Wrayback Farm, courtesy of Mr and Mrs George Robinson, who generously provided refreshments for the large and enthusiastic field before hounds, hunted by John Hardy, moved off to draw Breakback Wood.

Two spirited cubs gave hounds a good run-around before being accounted for by a newly entered hound, Rafter, of whom Mr Hardy had, he told us, expected great things.

Mr Hardy had intended to lift hounds and draw Garnerstone Copse, but before he could do so the day took an unexpected turn.

A large dog fox, his face clearly blood-stained, ran south out of Breakback Wood in the direction of the church at Bryandon.

He had a good lead on the nearest hound, Rafter's dam, Rachel, but nonetheless it was curious to see him come to a dead stop next to one of the mounted followers. He appeared to look up at the rider, and only broke away when Rachel, at the head of the pack, was a few feet away.

There was no stopping now, and the field were treated to a five-mile point (which was not at all what many of the novice riders had expected), before the fox was finally rolled over on the level crossing at Buckler's Gap. A train crossed the level crossing shortly afterwards. 'That train was late,' said the Master, Mrs Gage. 'And thank God it was. Had it been on time it would have been carnage.'

Although major disaster was averted it was a sad day for the hunt, and particularly for Mr Hardy. He had noticed that Rafter was not with the pack as the dog fox went away. She was later found dead in Breakback Wood, her throat badly bitten.

'A terrible day for the hunt,' said Mr Hardy. 'Rafter was the stuff of legend.' He would not comment on the likely cause of death.

ORCA

Orcinus orca

She cried out in the cold sea for company. It was also a lament because, as she knew, there was no possibility now of any company. But knowledge and hope occupy different domains in the heads of sophisticated creatures like orcas and humans.

The cry was in an arcane dialect now spoken by no one but her. The Icelanders who sometimes trailed south, and the cosmopolitan wanderers of the heaving Atlantic, knew it as the talk of orcas, and knew by the tone that it had to do with loss and desolation, but could not translate the details. Pain and pathos are always in the details: in the broken spectacles on the roadside, in the colour of the candles on the birthday cake, in the way your father tied his shoelaces, in the way that your grandmother taught you the sea-roads, in your mother's strange choice of commands when the fishermen tried to stab your calf with a harpoon, in your sister's curious last meal – a gannet snatched as it dived into a cloud of herring.

She had had a long life – many decades – in the valleys and on the mountain-tops between what humans call the islands – the dull damp deserts that rear from the sea off the coast of north-west Scotland. There are no fish and no seals in these deserts. The biggest trees are stunted rowans, naked in the winter. Her ancestors had tried the land and then, in disgust, about fifty million years ago, waddled back into the sea, from which, ever after, when they rose to blow and breathe, they had looked in pitying disbelief at the stranded humans.

The pity was real. It had in it none of the corrosive, self-congratulatory condescension that humans often call pity. Cetaceans sense the pain of a haddock and the angst of a strand of bladderwrack. Their pods move as single emotional units through the oceans, swimming in a pool of collective consciousness, tethered to one another by a mystic web of fizzing sensation and concern. If one breaks a bone in a flipper, the cousins feel it as an ache, and the mother as a stab. Since they know, as Darwin did, that there are no real boundaries between species, they feel the broken flippers and the broken spirits of humans too. No dolphin would ever rip a human baby away from its mother, lock it in a pitch-dark wardrobe inside an aeroplane, fly it ten thousand miles, and torture it until it did tricks in front of popcorn-eating audiences.

Our orca (really a big dolphin) felt the memories of her life and her dead in her body. She did not doze musingly in an armchair, seeing ghosts as we do. As she idled in a valley ten miles west of Skye, she swam again in her head the journey she had taken since childhood.

Her first memory was of touch: her mother's flipper stroking her head. They were in a safe place – tucked under a rocky overhang in deep green water somewhere off South Uist. Her mother stroked her head, and ribbons of weed stroked the rest of her body. Her aunt pressed in close, and her grandmother played with a dead seal pup, juggling it from nose to tail.

Of the senses we lumpen, truncated animals recognize, touch and sound were always the most important for her negotiation with the world. Sight was useless in the depths and whenever the algae bloomed in the happy trenches between the islands – trenches throbbing with flesh, where the orcas often hunted. But in the day and in the shallows, however blooming the water, there was always rocking above and stillness or swinging below, and our orca watched the rocking or the stillness or the swinging, according to her mood, and as she watched her heart settled and her worries dissolved. At night she lay often on the surface watching the winking lights of the occasional island settlements and the sliding ships, and though the beat of the ships' engines jarred with her own pulse, the lights ignited in her a warm companionability. When storms drove in from the Atlantic and the others dived deep into the calm, she strained up above the waves to feel the rasp of wind, her face bearded with spume.

But she was shaped and located by the press of other bodies, by the rush of water over her head and down her flanks, by the weight of the fathoms, by the laciness of weed, by tiny and vast changes in temperature. And, even more, by the sob of surf on the long white beaches, the churn of sand, the grunt of rocks prised from their roots, the screech of gulls, the whirr of turbines, the slap of waves on jetties and ship bellies.

The first *defining* things she learned were the names – the vocal signatures – of the others in her clan. When they were apart they broadcast their names into the sea: 'This is me.' And the others replied 'This is me,' and the wide cold boundless sea suddenly had the warmth and structure of the personalities that swam in it. This is how our orca found out that she *was*, and *what* she was, for she learned that she was not the others, and saw *how* she was not the others. Only when we can say, 'You!' can we properly say, 'Me!'

She chose her own name – the name that she would speak out to the sea. Part of her name came from the names of others – and particularly the others close to her. As we inherit the surnames of our parents, so she grafted the root of her mother's signature into her own. But the rest was a riff around that theme.

She could not herself have detailed the influences that determined her name. How many of us can? But there was in it the clicking of a crab from her first day outside her mother, the plunk of a diving guillemot, the whoosh of a yacht's wastepipe, the flump of a seal hauling itself on to a rock, and the low buzz of the very deep blue.

All this and much more was orchestrated into her name. To the scientists who sometimes listened through dangling hydrophones, and who slowed down her name and watched it spike on their oscilloscopes, it sounded like *eeschinnnmotrsiiiiiiiiizshy-uomautmasgasgasogsaousagmsgasgafgsghshakshagslllllastasgasgas-thessssss*. Since she had a name, I will give her one too. Her real one is too complex and mysterious for humans, and even to use the start of it might dangerously and misleadingly suggest that we understand her. But I will risk it, and call her Eeschin.

The relationship between Eeschin and the other orcas in her clan was highly emotional. They would have died for one another, and sometimes did (and that, though it might have made genetic sense, didn't *feel* at all like a cold calculation). But the relationship was also highly informed and discursive. Far more *data* was shared than in any human relationships. A squirt of sound a few seconds long contained the information encoded in a human feature film, complete with soundtrack, subtitles and credits. Beside them, the most intense human hypersensitive, with the largest library, the fastest internet connection and the most efficient search engine, is a sensory pauper. Orcas live – if they're allowed – as long as humans, but squeeze far more living into their time.

If we choose to live in our memories, we live in gauze-walled shacks with floors of mist, and talk with anaemic wraiths. But orca memories are immovable dwellings of rock and salt, fit for heroes, full of bellowing, red-blooded, slashing, wooing things.

Eeschin now lived in her memories, shuttling between them just as she moved between hunting grounds.

Memory

She was a calf, cruising with her family off the west coast. It was summer, and she rolled on to her back to see the the sun rolling over the hills of Harris. The clouds were more definite, with harder edges, than the clouds in her world, but the light, though stronger than hers, was more amorphous. Down in the kelp forests there were long spikes of sun, as if from search-lights, and between the spikes was blue shade.

A car moved along the flat shoreside road, and the flatness was the most surprising thing of all. Nothing was flat in Eeschin's life: not even the ceiling of the sea, or the sand plains coursing up to the beach. And the car was so loud. It thudded and spat gobbets of noise which made the air foul and gobbets of smoke which made it foul in a different way. The car, a quarter of a mile away, sent through the sea tremors like the ones you feel when you're stabbing into a big shoal of mackerel.

The car stopped and a man got out and shouted something to another man inside the car. To Eeschin's ear what he shouted sounded very simple indeed. It wouldn't take long at all, she thought, to be fluent in that rudimentary language.

That was how she first thought of humans: as basic, yobbish creatures, living in a different, simpler kind of space, communicating using the rough, crass linguistic tools suited to their few dimensions of being; poor things, but things that did not wear their poverty with the dignity customary to the sea.

Memory 2

Then she was at her grandmother's side, learning the sea-roads. Her grandmother was eighty, her back pock-marked with weals from machine-gun bullets – courtesy of a bored sailor – in the Second World War. Behind her dorsal fin, which rose from the Sound like the black sail of a sinister racing yacht, the grandmother bore too the scar from a rifle bullet fired by a fisherman who thought that another orca with a mouthful of mackerel had taunted him for his empty nets.

She was a good pupil, her grandmother told her in a gush of Morse. Eeschin would inherit the mantle, and guide the clan from danger and to peace and plenty. The old ways were the best, Eeschin understood; the old roads, laid down thousands of years ago, hallowed by experience, and etched so deep into the huge brains of the clan members that departure from them was seen as offensive disloyalty. They have served us well, she was told – and 'us' meant the clan, living and dead, for the dead were not disenfranchised as they are for most humans, but a continuing, contributing presence. The dead lived not only in the roads they had made, the habits they had engrained and the genes they had bequeathed, but on the edges of sight and at the corners of words.

From her grandmother and her mother she learned the imperative of kindness and the grammar of relationship: the careful choreography of respect and the right inflections of exuberance: how and where to stroke; when and how to leap; the right and wrong ways to nuzzle; when compliment becomes sycophancy and ardour becomes lust. This was a genial but straitlaced clan, set in their ways, frowning on innovation, hospitable but rather stiff to outsiders – whether the outsiders were other cetaceans or unfamiliar ideas.

Memory 3

Eeschin with the other orcas, was again at her grandmother's side. They were all transparent to one another: they saw ultrasonic pictures of one another – the earnest ventricles, the fluttering valves, the remnants of a seal pup being squeezed along the colon, the tongue ramming a gannet down the gullet. But in her grandmother there was something new, something that shouldn't be there: a jagged mass in her belly which didn't move when her tubes squeezed the food along. The others clustered around, beckoning and pointing with their noses, and discussing. Several of the older ones, knowing how beams of sound could dissolve tension and erode kidney stones, shot ultrasound at the lump, trying to massage it away. The grandmother grunted and nodded appreciation, but shook her head and swam away. They followed her, as she secretly hoped they would. They followed her then and for the next three months as the flesh slipped off her, and they heard her final instructions to them (an intricate and highly conservative plan for the community). They followed her when she swam straight out to sea, and watched as she stopped swimming and dropped into the deepest valley within five hundred miles of South Uist.

Memory 4

Then Eeschin was with her mother, who now swam with a new, tired deliberation, no longer a mother, but a matriarch; no longer just Eeschin's mother, but the mother of the clan, too preoccupied for games; earnest and suddenly old, concerned about schooling, protocols and the finer points of grammar. Somehow, too, from the tone of concern, Eeschin knew that she would lead the clan herself one day, and so she was an earnest child, not jumping as high as her cousins or, as they did, messing around with squid before eating them, prising up stones in search of little brown fish, or masturbating luxuriously against big columns of kelp. Instead she became prissily censorious, tending to keep the company of adults, and tuttutting when she saw the cousins looking lustfully at the dashing Icelanders who sometimes came south.

Memory 5

Sex with the Icelanders – or with anyone outside the small clan – was impossible, and so, thought Eeschin, flirtation was a waste of time. It was impossible because sex was a serious business which could happen only in a committed relationship, in which both parties undertook the gruelling long-term obligations associated with parenthood. Such relationships involved *talking.* The Icelanders and Eeschin's West Coast community were separated from one another by impenetrable linguistic and hence cultural walls. They were genetically compatible – their gametes could fuse to form viable zygotes – but that was an irrelevance: they could never meet in the conditions regarded by orcas as essential for sex. They were further apart than Montagues and Capulets, Southern Baptists and Belzer Hasidim, or Amish and Software Engineers. No human cultural or linguistic hurdles are so high. Culture and language matter less to us, and human culture and language are less entangled.

For the West Coast community this meant incest or, at best, pairings with cousins who were themselves the offspring of cousins: cousins who often had odd-shaped flippers, lumpy foreheads, or teeth in the roof of their mouths.

Twice Eeschin had been elaborately courted: fed fish and made to listen to boasts about killing seals. Twice she had at last given in, and the pair shuddered together in mid-water, once off Ullapool with the sun streaming down and the others looking on without a snigger, and once off Scourie, as the sea's hide was thrashed with hail and the sea bled spume which washed over their backs when they finished and rose to the surface to breathe.

After each of these times Eeschin knew a fullness inside her, couldn't stomach mackerel for a while, and wanted to eat crabs, which she normally hated. But the first fullness melted quietly away, and though the second fullness lasted longer, she at last felt griping pain and forced out a dead calf which had the look, so she thought, of her grandmother.

Eeschin couldn't let her grandmother sink again, as she had done five years before, and she sensed too, but vaguely, that if she let the calf sink she would sink herself. So for eight increasingly smelly weeks she nudged the calf around between Barra and Harris, snapping at the gulls which swooped to peck at it and diving with it in her jaws when boats came near. But she couldn't see off the bacteria, and the calf lost the look of its great-grandmother. Eeschin's guard dropped, and one November day a fisherman on Harris, looking from his cottage window, saw a white raft of squabbling gulls, and circling slowly round it, a tall sail fin which finally peeled off and headed due west into the dying sun.

Memory 6

Her mother was dead, mangled by the screw of a container ship which had made her brain boil up out of her skull and nearly sliced off her dorsal fin. That screw reshaped the whole clan's world. All orcas experience a prolonged grief which in humans would be called pathological. The death of a matriarch subdued them all for ever. The sea was never so blue again. Seal liver never had its old taste. They learned new accents of lament which they used for sad, confused arias, sometimes with five or six parts. Their speech and their jumps were flat, they sometimes groomed one another manically and sometimes forgot to groom at all. If they'd had clothes they'd have looked dishevelled. They smiled less, and the youngsters thought their parents were no fun at all.

For Eeschin the distress was particularly keen, but she sublimated it into busyness, which prolonged it. She was now in charge. She did not have the healing luxury of active mourning. Her mother would never have let her own feelings get in the way of her responsibility to the clan, and Eeschin was her mother's daughter. The greater the distress of the others, the more important it was for Eeschin to be stalwart. If all around was changing, all the more reason to be steady.

Steadiness meant fealty to the old ways, to the edicts of the ancestors. But that wasn't so easy.

Memory 7

Hunters need to be ecologists, eavesdropping on the discourse between prey and place. Few places provide sufficient bounty throughout the year, especially for big-bodied animals, and so hunters need to align their seasons with the seasons of the food: they need calendars and inside information. If you weigh two and a half tonnes you don't just happen to bump into sufficient calories. You need to know when the salmon will mass in the estuaries, waiting to climb the rivers; when the seal pups will launch off the rocks; when the mackerel will be running in the lochs; when that minke whale you saw mating last autumn will produce her calf; when the silver eels will gush with the storm-water from the hills of Ross towards fulfilment and death in the Sargasso.

Eeschin had learned these patterns beside her mother and grandmother. They were ancient and powerful patterns, repre-sented in her head as perfectly jointed pieces, together making a whole in which she lived and moved and had her being. She had a carpenter's joy in making them fit so tightly that no one in the clan could see the joints. She wanted the others to feel the seamlessness of the sea. She knew that if there were visible seams fear and division would seep through and infect the clan – already fragile with grief.

But things were changing. She led her clan one August to a deep cold loch, overhung with oak and overlooked by deer. Every August for ever the loch had shivered with mackerel. 'You could walk across on them,' said one old man, remembering his childhood. For at least a month the loch was not dark, but alight with mackerel backs, and did not look deep, because if you stared down from the side of your boat your face was reflected back to you from their scales, twisted in a hall of mirrors.

But this summer they were not there, and the loch was as deep and dark as in December. Eeschin looked everywhere. She dived to the bottom and thrashed the silt in frustration. This could not be. Mackerel in that loch in August were as axiomatic for orcas as the proposition that $2 + 2 = 4$ is for us. If the mackerel were not there the whole weave of the world would start to unravel.

When most things are going well we don't notice the niggles – or they are stored in some dusty filing cabinet of our minds. It is the same for orcas.

As Eeschin swam from the loch towards the open sea, her mind trying to recalibrate itself to a reality where $2 + 2 \neq 4$, she remembered that the boundary between the warm and the cold water in the Minch – previously as flat as a billiard table – had recently started to crumple. Hot and cold were getting mixed up. She'd dismissed it, but perhaps it meant something.

She remembered too that the sea grass looked thinner. It gave back less of a signal, and there were bald patches.

Once she started remembering, the last couple of decades seemed to be pock-marked with anomalies. Now she came to think of it, the anomalies weren't anomalies at all: they *were* the new sea.

For years there had been no seal pups on the rock she called *ioooltiiiiczx*. The seabed along the coast of Knoydart was coated in thin pale fur. There were only occasional tiny cod. Where were the herring? Some of the lobsters had a third claw growing out of their back. You couldn't see six inches in front of your face by the pipe that spills out by *hjliyusrsss*, and in the summer even sonar struggled to pierce the soup. An octopus off *oiklssssstyzx* went mad and jetted out from behind its rock and plastered itself to Eeschin's head: others were depressed and hovered in plain sight, waiting to be eaten.

And the tastes? Even allowing for the distortions of nostalgia, as the wise Eeschin did, the tastes weren't what they had been. The fish were less fishy, the seals less sealy. Both had a touch of tin, and made her big hard gums pucker and twitch.

The sea-roads, she now noted (keeping the insight to herself) had changed. Sometimes, now, they cut across the grain of the sea rather than curving gently with it, and the sea itself sometimes seemed to protest. Something was happening that set the sea against the community.

Memory 8

August again, a year later. The community was divided for a while: some off the coast of Antrim, some, with Eeschin, off the northern tip of Skye, wallowing at the surface, nibbling, winking and fondling, happy to feel the sun on their backs and lumps of a big old seal in their bellies.

Then a sudden banging, which they felt all the way round their bodies and through their heads, as humans feel if they're standing right in front of huge speakers at a rock concert, but far more intense, for they could pick up the flutter of a whiting at a hundred yards. It got louder and closer, so that they might have been in a tight tin box with a thousand sledgehammers pounding it on every side. They had no fingers to stick in their ears.

They knew what it was. They knew that if they stayed the boat engines would be switched off and instead they'd hear the click of cameras, the ping of phones and sips of air, which is what the humans call breathing – though it isn't at all like the great tides of salt air and hill air that surge in and out of cetaceans.

If the orcas moved off, the boat would chase them, and though they could outpace it easily enough, they couldn't be bothered. So they stayed, rolling and blowing, feeling that the boat was ill-mannered. It drifted closer, which was even more ill-mannered, and people hung over the edge. Eeschin lifted her head and shot a wad of ultrasound at them and knew from the echoes that one of the females would soon be dead.

The doomed human female held the flipper of a human calf. Eeschin liked that. So she swam closer, right up to the boat, and there was now complete silence on the boat apart from the cameras, and it didn't seem as if the humans were breathing at all. Eeschin now used her eyes, and with her right eye, which was the best one, she looked at the calf who would soon lose her mother, and gave a screech of pity and consolation that was five octaves higher than even the calf, whose hearing was uncompromised by decades of acoustic violence, could hear. The calf, though, looked Eeschin full in that one eye with her own two brown ones. The calf's face went a strange shape, and Eeschin thought she must have understood. Encouraged, she gave the calf the whole liturgy of lament and reassurance, and then the calf threw a cup of hot tea in her eye.

Memory 9

When the tide crept in, the weed, which had been lying flat on the rock, rose on its bladders into a cathedral of swaying green pillars with a roof of splintered sun.

Dog-faced grey seals, bored with lying out on the islands, bent like blotchy bananas, and scared of the packs of hunters on the plains of the open sea, came often for refuge to the cathedral, and to play hide and seek between the pillars.

Seal flesh was good. Good, too, for a person like Eeschin, who was as interested in frontiers as we are in celebrity scandal, was the lisping conversation between the land and the sea – a conversation that humans call the shore. The rasp of shingle reminded her of the time when her race decided to return to the sea from which everything had come and to which everything would return. She pulled up her head, rested her chin on a rock, and stared inland.

She saw blue peat smoke curling up from a croft at the water's edge as fish milt smokes into the sea from male vents at mating time. She saw an otter working along the line of wrack, turning over oiled seabirds with his paw, and knew how the otter would taste. She saw the waves in the tall meadow behind the croft as the wind came in from the ocean, and wanted to swim through them. She saw a stag, thin and tired from keeping his harem, and thought he was a fine fellow, for he knew as she did about responsibility. She did not know that he cared only for himself and for the future of his traits once he was dead, and would have been disgusted if she had.

She saw the rocks on the shore, ablaze with lichen, and primroses on a bank that climbed into a wood, and beyond that a quiet land; a place of pastels, blends, slopes and gentle transitions. The mountains were smaller and less abrupt than hers. The caves, she imagined, had fewer teeth than the sea-caves. She saw no herds of scavengers. The gulls gave up as the wood started. The inland birds were stately, gliding like confident skate.

Two humans walked slowly along the distant strand, flipper in flipper, not hunting, hiding, searching or even talking. Eeschin's tall sail fin was obvious, but the humans' heads were bent down and they did not see her, smell her, or hear the puff of her occasional breaths. They wouldn't survive a moment in the sea, thought Eeschin, and felt protective, though she hadn't forgotten the hot tea.

Nothing much seemed to happen on the land. It was a muffled, muted place, with no real highs or lows; a place to sleep, perhaps, but not to live. Indeed how *could* anyone live there? What would they eat? Eeschin ate no plants, but she guessed that the hard-cased trees and the dry gnarled stalks of heather would be harder to chew even than the most rubbery trunks of the sea. And where was the flesh? The stag would not keep anyone going for long, and since she had seen flocks of humans together, from apparently different families, she presumed that they did not eat one another – at least not often. She herself would feel uneasy about eating humans. She wasn't sure why. She supposed they would taste all right – though from what she'd seen their diet was junk. Her world was full of taboos like that; taboos of ancient and obscure origin, their power increased by age and obscurity.

She slid her chin from the rock, wanting again the huge and intimate sea; the sea that crowded round her head, crackling, humming and gossiping; the sea of twisting light and proper darkness.

She went slowly along the coast, hanging over the cliff that fell three hundred feet to a pool that turned once a month and, though they didn't know it, regulated the menstrual cycles of the women in the chip shop on the quay.

Beyond the little grey town, out of the tourists' sight, a ceramic pipe led into the water, and by its mouth big fish swallowed small fry that lived on the dense clouds of dung. Many of these big fish were intersex, bearing both male and female genitals. They would have been males but for the human reproductive hormones in the sea water.

Eeschin went there to hunt, usually taking a companion or two with her. There was always food, and her poor sense of smell made it bearable, but it never felt right.

Today she was on her own. She had had a six-foot conger eel, but with its last gasp, as it disappeared tail first inside her, it had bitten her tongue and held on and taken some dislodging. Now Eeschin was sore and cross, and the eel was still thrashing down below, making her liverish, so she had risen to the surface to splash around and take her mind off her mouth.

There was a crack from the shore, and a thud and a sting on her dorsal fin, but since this made no sense she only jerked, and did not dive. Another thud: another sting. This time behind her head. She tasted her own blood in the water along with the shit and the condoms, but this was simply interesting, and she stayed on the surface to find out what was happening.

From the quay of the women who were synchronized with the underwater whirlpool came a buzzing and a thudding and a whining which hurt Eeschin far more than the bullets, for they burrowed into her brain and streamed like fire along her back.

The boat bounced and slapped in its desperation to get near Eeschin. The desperation had nothing to do with worry about fish stocks. Fishermen do kill orcas – even omnivorous orcas like Eeschin who increase fish numbers by eating fish-eating seals. But it wasn't a fisherman at the helm; these were City boys up (or, as they'd say, down) from London, staying at the big house, who'd learned from the movies the 'yee-har' that now whooped across the sea. Unlike Eeschin, they weren't prone to or equipped for introspection, but had they been they would have struggled to account for their actions. For there were no reasons, and nothingness is hard to describe, and so gets away with a lot for which it should be pilloried. Perhaps, though – although this doesn't count as a reason – it had something to do with affronted pride. Perhaps at some level – though they were short on levels – they realized that Eeschin was better than they were: faster, kinder, wiser, stronger, more knowledgeable, more resourceful, more moral. And perhaps they knew that male orcas have far, far longer penises than they did.

Their first pass across Eeschin's back ploughed a furrow into her muscle, two inches deep and three feet long. Their second, after they'd spun the boat, crossed the first furrow, leaving a hole down which sea water gurgled to the very edge of her pleural cavity. On their third (they were excited now by the reddening froth), the upstroke of Eeschin's tail as she dived in pain and panic flipped the boat over, catapulting the men into the air, and the downstroke slapped two of them head first on to the underside of the boat. One died then; the other's life-support machine was switched off a month later in the Inverness hospital.

The survivor sold the story of the man-killing orca to the press, became a hero, appeared on breakfast TV, and gathered a posse of lantern-jawed hard men who stayed in Skye's finest hotel, rented boats mounted with exploding harpoons to search for the homicidal rogue, drank the bar dry, and soon crept back to wherever people like that come from.

Eeschin went to the Faroes with a solicitous friend to heal.

Memory 10

The hole closed. The furrows filled. But Eeschin now began to draw conclusions about humans. To judge. She became that very rare thing – a cynical, misanthropic orca. She thought often about humans. Their marks were everywhere. A calf was snagged in an abandoned net and drowned. A rack of deafening turbines was built into the tidal race where the most succulent seals loved to hunt. A tanker broke its back on a reef. Its oil killed seabirds for five hundred miles, made Eeschin asthmatic, and killed from pneumonia the last calf the community was ever to have. The survivors all had dermatitis and rubbed themselves raw against barnacle-covered rock. Effluent spewed from ships made them cough and made their eyes sting. Giggling sightseers in glass-bottomed boats violated the grave proprieties of the sea, whose joy depends on absolute seriousness.

For Eeschin, as for most humans that have ever lived, the

cosmos teemed with agency. Everything had a cause, everything *could* cause, everything had the dignity of causation, and so Eeschin swam through a thick rich stew of causation and responsibility. It meant that whenever she was satisfied about a cause, she was severe in her judgement of the actor, for she knew that the actor was free, and need not have acted in that way.

She was not sure about some causes. She did not know why the currents were scrambled, the reefs dead, the great whales gone, the summer sea a rubber rug of jellyfish, the seals panting and decrepit, the rocks coated with brown-green slime. But she did know the power, the ubiquity, the carelessness, the vulgarity and the cruelty of humans, and she could draw inferences. Her instinctive goodwill was corroded by the acid rain that fell in sheets, bringing the reek of heavy industry into the tides and the spindrift and making the shells of the crustaceans and the molluscs flabby.

But this is no tale of an orca gone rogue; of retributive violence that you might applaud or deplore, but which at least you would understand. Eeschin might have made a career and a name for herself by hounding the humans. Humans were, after all, often pitiably vulnerable, dithering on the fringe of the sea in the summer, sinking clumsily into the depths with humps on their backs and glass on their faces, or fussing about in tiny boats in the hope of hauling in a few mackerel on feathered hooks. Humans were edible enough. It made no common sense not to eat them, but still the old uncommon sense prevailed, and Eeschin's resentment took the shape of a simmering disappointment in the humans. What might they have been! What might they still be! What times they could have together, guiding one another round their respective caves and woods and different ways of being in the world. Her heart beat faster when she heard a distant boat, and then she slumped into sullenness. She usually dived deep and stayed down when humans were abroad – not out of fear, but distaste – but sometimes she surfaced briefly behind a boat where she knew the humans were unlikely to see her, and looked balefully at it, wondering if the child with the cup of tea was aboard, and if so whether the child might explain herself.

There came a moment when Eeschin noticed that she preferred the winter. That moment was her tenth memory-dwelling.

Perhaps this was her age. The pleasures of tango-ing with sunbeams and blowing the salt cream from the edge of hot waves are fine as far as they go, but they pall because they are not perennial, and age demands, before it is too late, things that will last.

That was not the whole story. There was a growing seriousness in Eeschin; a seriousness which, since it was not shared by the other members of her community, left her lonely. The summer was blithe, and so were the others, and she was not. Responsibility had forced her to realize the complexity of the sea and the earnestness of its discussion with the land. The earnestness was loudest when the sea piled up darkly and rolled rocks the size of cars like marbles and plucked miles of seabed and flung it into the woods and threw boats across roads and through walls into kitchens and split seals and powdered shells and kept humans cowering in their holes and made the clouds run like terrified whitebait. And when she heard this she said to herself – though not in Morse, for that was for others: Yes, this is how it is.

Memory 11

The winter made her notice. Suddenly, one dark February afternoon, just after she had surfaced in the middle of a group of guillemots sleeping on the swinging sea. She noticed that there had been no calves for twelve summers. She noticed that the group swam half the distance in a year than it had, swam more slowly, and did not explode on to seals as they once did. She noticed that several of the group had visible necks, for the fat had gone. She noticed that long dives were rare, that the old deep idling spots – the hallowed community halls – had been unused for years, and that the talk proper to such places – the telling and embellishment of the old stories – had not happened since the last calf.

She blamed herself for not noticing earlier, and blamed herself for noticing now, for the noticing seemed to accelerate the evil. This was probably not so. Probably, as the group grew thinner, the polychlorinated biphenyls, polybrominated diphenyl ethers and poisonous metals, long locked up in their fat, were leaching out into their circulation, their psyches, their livers and their kidneys, turning their stomachs, draining their appetites, switching off their hormones, abating their libido and truncating their zest. And also they were paying the price of their intimacy, parochialism and cultural isolation. Since they could speak only with and woo only one another, their pairings would have been genetically doomed even if their sperm and eggs had been viable.

It was too late now to learn new dialects or mores, even had that been psychologically possible. For centuries it had been unthinkable. The imperative of clinging to the ways of the ancestors trumped the imperative of reproduction, and only now did Eeschin understand that their devotion to the old ways meant that they would not be ancestors themselves; that the old ways would die with them.

This could not be borne unless it was turned into epic. The summer had no epic, but the winter storms did, and Eeschin became a wintry thing, distant and tight-lipped. In her wodges of sound there were now no serenades, jokes or invitations, but only directions. The epic by which she lived was a shrivelled, stoic story of duty, endurance, and the fate encoded in the lurch and smash of a wave.

Memory 12

Once you start noticing things there's no way back. It takes you over. You become a noticer, and unless the noticing is done with the right kind of attention it can unmake you. You can shrink to become just the things you see.

Eeschin shrank as she noticed; shrank until she was just a hard cold core of winter, habits, duties and convictions. Having become a noticer, she noticed all the more, and shrank more and became harder and colder.

The necks of the clan got stringy. Then, all of a sudden, the older ones started to sag: there is no other word for it. Eeschin alone was preserved, for in orcas, as in humans, testing dutiful caring prevents degeneration as no amount of rest or medication can do. She felt this; felt the preservative power in her of the old stories, and sought to stop the decay of the community by injecting story.

The sustaining stories were about place and the claim of

place on their ancestors. Of the way that the grey geese had shown the way through the sea; of seals who became women and tried to lure the community into a narrow throat of rock from which they'd never escape, and how the rock shouted to warn of the plan; of a trench so deep that you could swim down it for a month, yet was always full of sun, and where the salmon were the size of seals and counted it an honour to die; of a gannet who knew the speech of the clan and told of ice cliffs, black beaches and flotillas of flightless puffins so dense that you could fill your stomach by swimming at the surface with an open mouth; and of an old lady – perhaps a thousand years old – who led her clan to the other side of the world and back each year, and how they ate fish the colour of shattered light and turned from black and white to the colours of the rainbow; and how the bones of all orcas are rolled and polished at the bottom of the sea and then – though it might take some time – gathered together in a mountain the size of the inverted peak off South Uist, and how something then happens to them. But just what, no one other than the dead elders themselves knows.

Eeschin was right: these stories were necessary for survival, and they could stave off death for a while. But they too gave way to the pesticides.

One by one the orcas slipped away. Slipping is just how it was. The calls got quieter and more colourless. There was no agonizing; no raging against the dying of the light. Had the others been themselves they would have raged; would have refused to let go; would have borne the ailing one up so that its blowhole was always above the waves; would have stroked away the malaise and scanned the body with their ultrasound and tried to smash up the culprit that was consuming from inside. But there was nothing to see, and they were too tired themselves, and so each orca fell further behind, started to inhale water, and after blowing and panting, slipped down and down, first through the green and then through blue and then through the dark, to be picked clean and join the bone-mountain and rejoin their parents and, for all we know, their own unborn calves too.

Memory 13

Now Eeschin was on her own, but she kept talking, because you never know. She kept on broadcasting beams of sound to the sea, and they came back to her, telling her what was there. This was a real conversation, and she found it a comfort. One beam would hit a strand of coral, and the coral sent back a picture of itself. One would ricochet between the bladders in a field of wrack, and the wrack returned a complex grid which it was happily distracting to decode. Each returned sound had a flavour for her. Limestone-sound tasted different from granite-sound, and seal-sound from whale-sound. The world gave back to her an honest account of itself. Eeschin's sound tunnelled far beneath the skin of rocks and fish. She did not interpret it as we interpret the data that stream into our eyes – she had the humility to believe that rocks knew more about themselves than she did. So she lived in the world that really existed rather than, as we do, in a dowdier self-made world.

This meant that even when the others were dead, Eeschin was not alone. She had, as we do not, a real relationship, founded on real knowledge, with the things she irradiated with her sound. Our loneliness is complete when, however crowded the room, we realize that we are talking only with ourselves; that we have long been locked into the echo chamber of our own head, and that escape is near impossible. That moment comes often for us at death or, if we're lucky, rather earlier, when, just occasionally, panic propels us out of our heads and into a real rapport with someone or something else.

Eeschin did not panic. She was cocooned, as she always had been, by the sea and all that was in it.

There was a year of maudlin peace, unencumbered but also unenhanced by obligation. She was not needed now, except in the sense that we are each needed because each death diminishes all. She swam the old routes; always calling. She swam between Barra and South Uist, and from Uig down to the tip of Loch Hourn, hearing the bellow of stags on the mountains of Skye, watching lightning crack between the tops on the Cuillin ridge, feeling in her bowels the rumbling of the great whales hunting squid in the Sound.

But most of all she swam between these thirteen memories. They were like ports for her. Once she had been conscious of the journey between them: the ports had been strung together by a chain that related in some way to what she *was*. Now the chain had rotted from long exposure to sea water, grief and heavy metals, and I do not know if it is right to say that *Eeschin* continued to do the swimming – though an orca looking very like her, with scars on her head and her back, was seen for many more years by fishermen off the west coast of Scotland.

But since I cannot be sure that this was the same orca, I must end this story now.

HUMAN

Homo sapiens

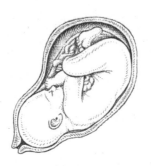

Under goose feathers, on a stormy autumn night, after the ingestion of alcohol made by fungi from plant sugars, and when there was nothing good on the TV, two gametes fused to form a zygote. The zygote had Norsemen, Arabs, Spaniards, Greeks, English, African, Neanderthal, Plesiosaur, bivalves and amoeba on her mother's side, and French, Chinese, Dutch, African, Neanderthal, Plesiosaur, bivalves and amoeba on her father's. She buried herself in a plush red cell-forest, and the cells closed welcomingly over her.

When, before breakfast a few weeks later, she made her presence felt, her mother was not as welcoming as the cells had been, but the embryo survived the dose of more plant-based alcohol the mother half hoped would evict her, and started to borrow her mother's blood supply. The mother's resentment changed to wonder and fear. The embryo grew fingers and began to clap, and grew toes and began to kick. She heard the B Minor Mass as a distant rumour, and, as the metronome giving her the pace of life, the swoosh-aaaah, swoosh-aaaah of her mother's blood.

As most of her ancestors had been, she was now a deep-sea creature, squatting in pitch dark water with the same osmolarity as the Mediterranean. The sea was more tidal than the Mediterranean, and the tides more erratic, but it had similar noises: cracklings, scrapings and screams. She drank the sea, and voided into it. All her efforts – and they were many – were directed towards escaping the sea. She kicked against the sea wall, trying to break it down. Her chest heaved, practising for air, though her lungs were useless, stuck together like a wet, collapsed balloon. Her skin was white, waterlogged and corrugated from the marinade. Her eyes had known no light, but when she pressed her fists against her eyeballs she saw bright patterns and showers of sparks, as she would when she died. This amused her, and she spent many of her waking hours exploring the grids and the lacework and watching the fireworks. Her dependence was total and, knowing this, her mother cradled the bulge, gave up tobacco and, eventually, her job, and took up meditation and organic food. Once a week she met with other gravid females at gatherings where, over decaffeinated tea, they fuelled their neuroses and stoked their fears.

The mother's (occasional) partner, helped by a pretty young thing from telesales, pretended it wasn't happening. But when the sea wall was finally breached and the mother's waters broke over the front passenger seat of the Fiesta like a hot winter storm over an Ushant lighthouse, he couldn't pretend any more, and drove the car, now awash, to the local hospital.

There, despite her earlier desperation to leave, the child now tried desperately to stay. She was of the light at the end of the tunnel, of the clank of metal instruments, of the barked commands, of the pressure that was like the pressure three hundred metres down on the seabed. She could not resist the squeeze, but her shoulders, wedged and immovable, could. Her head, going blue and then black, hung out in the halogen glare and the air and the gas and the clamour and the haze of antiseptic spray; her body, blue now too, and floppy, lay in the dark sea.

A woman pressed mercilessly on the mother's abdomen. Another hooked her finger under the child's chin, grabbed her head with rubber-gloved hands, twisted and pulled. The shoulders popped free and the child slithered out in a rush of splendid yolk-yellow meconium and steaming faeces and was swung round the midwife's head and slapped on the back to get her going because those were the good old days. The child and the mother were both suddenly alone and would be alone for ever and would slowly come to know it.

Clever people thereafter differed, as they peered at brain scans in multidisciplinary team meetings, about the significance of that amphibious time in the child's life – part in, part out of the sea. Most connected it to the shambling, knock-kneed gait, the head-tilt, the squint and the slurred speech. Many thought it responsible for her woeful performance in tests designed to assess how efficiently the subject could forge and follow algorithms and make money. And a few, off the record, wondered if it was connected with the child's insistence that she could talk to the birds in the hospital garden, watch the top of her own head, see objects through walls, stop clocks by looking at them, and feel the pain of others. Her descriptions of the world were crowded and exuberant. If she could be believed, epiphanies jostled merrily and sang out laughingly for attention, sparrows glowed like birds of paradise, and angels drove along the bypass in chariots of fire. The drugs they gave her to abolish these visions made her less able to describe them in her therapy sessions; it is not clear that they restored her to whatever her right mind was, for she continued to write delusional poems in the style of Blake, and to smile when there was nothing at all to smile about.

A very old psychotherapist, too old to care what people thought, wrote on the file:

I saw———in the clinic today. My impression is that, as Aldous Huxley would have said, the brain's reducing valve is much slacker than in most subjects. There is a massive flow of data into the brain, resulting in the subject's view of the world being constructed using much more information than in most people. This is supposed to make humans mad – hence the valve to reduce the flow to a manageable dribble. I see no signs of pathology here. Quite the opposite. This child is one of the epistemological elite, and so will have a hard time living among epistemological cripples like me.

His contract was not renewed.

The mother was devastated but dutiful. She kept the child, lost the father, and was alternately cheered and spooked by the constant smiling.

The child knew, better than we do, the sort of place this is, and so could be more at home here than we are; could see that sparrows really do shimmer.

She rarely chose to walk on hind legs. That was not because of her peculiar gait, but because she didn't want to miss the information pouring in through her hands; because she knew that unless she touched *that* worm cast, *that* oak leaf and *that* starling's tibia, she would not know the garden, and because she knew that eyes did not give real knowledge. She needed and wanted knowledge *of*, not knowledge *about* – which is all, at the very best, that eyes can give.

She wanted her eyes to be down there on the ground, corroborating, contradicting or playing counterpoint around whatever it was that her palms and her nose and her beetle-licking tongue and her intuitions about her family relationships with beetles told her.

She heard the green in the new grass; saw the brown smell of a decaying mole; tasted the trill at the end of a whitethroat's morning salute (and her tongue slowed the trill down, so that each note could be tasted); smelt the high blue where the swifts played; stroked a badger's cough; was kicked, mocked and parodied; and she liked to bake shortbread.

She knew when the swallows in Malawi turned north, when they were chewed by a storm over the Congo, and, to the minute – because she knew the southward tug in her own chest – when they would leave. She smelt the click of a centipede's joints and the spicy uncurling of a woodpecker's tongue. She put her fingers and sometimes her head through cave walls and laughed in recognition when she found what was on the other side. She knew the prime numbers up to two million (though she couldn't remember quite all of their names), but was no good at long division and couldn't understand the bad-mannered way copper behaved when it met concentrated sulphuric acid. She didn't get shops, was arrested many times, and sat smiling before a befuddled probation officer.

Her mother fed her, housed her, asked why this had happened, had her own womb out in case it happened again, and started a business so that she had a proper outlet for her care and attention.

The child took up painting, and after a month of bushes and trees with human faces, the mother could take no more, dumped her in the car and drove her to a community where, she told her friends, they dealt with weird stuff. But they didn't. Not really. If working in the community's café didn't work, they were at a loss.

It didn't work.

The café faced a bank, a chip shop, some charity shops and a row of bus stops. There was no view of the sky from the front of the café. At the back, as the child washed up, she looked out at a wall that even her hands could not penetrate, for at the other side was a dry cleaner's. There was no lichen on the wall: it was clean as a mortician's slab.

She had her own windowless room between one of the staff helpers, who wanted to be an office manager, and a sixteen-year-old video-game addict who ate heaped tablespoons of instant coffee to stop himself sleeping. The air and water were filtered; the only permitted alcohol was for swabbing the taps and the toilet flushes. The cats, like the child's mother, were spayed. There was no darkness or cold in winter, no intrusive light or heat in summer, and no silence. The road, running between a hospital and an industrial estate, snarled and flashed through the night. There was a small lawn, the manager's delight, a perfect monoculture, sprayed thrice-yearly, trimmed and strimmed three-weekly and never, ever walked on. The cats, though fat from barrenness and tinned fish, still managed to kill birds, which they left on the child's pillow. The child grew fat on white bread and imported noodles, and would not paint.

She moped, they said in the café. There were complaints. She was moved to the back room. She dropped plates – some said deliberately – and when a customer sent back a blood-stained fork (a curious thing in a vegetarian café), the manager noticed a series of fresh cuts on the child's arms.

There was of course an inquiry, with sheaves of forms, many earnest meetings, and an assurance of reference to the 'appropriate statutory agencies'. The child smiled for the first time in months when asked to complete a psychological profiling questionnaire, but the smile was like the Archaic smile on Greek stone faces rather than the smile she used to give to robins, and there wasn't a box on the form for that.

The upshot was that the child, who was now chronologically and hormonally an adult, stayed where she was, washing up, cutting lemon drizzle cake into squares, going early to bed and to sleep smiling the Archaic smile that had never left her lips since the questionnaire. She wore a bracelet she had plaited from the strands of a woollen rug and, underneath, another bracelet that broadcast her position to the manager's phone.

There was no more cutting. It had been a phase, the six-month review concluded: all stakeholders were congratulated on a timely and successful intervention.

One April day the child disappeared. The electronic bracelet was found in the toilet cistern. CCTV showed the child opening the front door just after dawn, raising her head to look east, inhaling deeply, and closing the door quietly before walking confidently away. An early-morning jogger recalled a smiling child sitting under a tree in a park a couple of miles away, feeding jackdaws with bread from its backpack. A policeman, later reprimanded for his low index of suspicion, had seen a thin figure limping towards the bus station, trailing a teddy bear and eating a carrot. A bus driver clearly recollected a 'simple-looking kid' who asked to go to 'the big wood on the hill', because she paid a £2 fare with a £20 note.

The harassed and outraged manager, to add to his woes, had to answer some searching questions about why all the petty cash had been left in a now absent cash box on his desk. A farmer, doing the rounds of his stock on his quad bike, remembered, now you come to mention it, an improbable hiker picking her way up a sunken lane to a stand of oak while being mobbed, it seemed to him, by magpies, 'just like an old owl, but friendly, like'. A local naturalist with poetic aspirations emailed the police station about a 'wan, elfin thing gazing, just gazing at the tree tops, and sometimes beckoning'. He didn't know what to think. 'I wondered if it was one of those Eastern rituals: what do you call it? Tai chi?'

And a poacher, wandering the hedgerow with a gun and a discreet dog, hadn't seen anything at all, had he, because he was miles away, wasn't he, watching the football – on his own, sadly – and certainly hadn't seen any freaky kid cover itself at sundown with the last of the winter leaves and lie with just its strange peaky face poking out, looking at the first bats of the season flickering between the twigs. Anyway, if he'd gone back in the morning to check snares, which of course he didn't, he'd have seen no sign of the child apart from a trail of footprints in the mud leading to the top of the wood and then down into the vale.

A hastily convened crisis meeting concluded, to everyone's relief, that there was no crisis. The legal advice was clear: the centre was not at fault, and bore no continuing responsibility. The child was not a child at all, but a capacitous if rather eccentric adult. The centre was not a prison. The child was free to come and go as she pleased, and if it pleased her to go and not to come again, that was her constitutional right as a citizen of this great country, and there was nothing that anyone could or should try to do about it. The police liaison inspector, relieved, closed his file and redeployed his search team to the job of arresting school kids and university professors who had locked themselves to railings outside an arms trade exhibition.

So the child was left to roam free. It is impossible to piece together a complete picture of her movements. There are only isolated reports. They agree that April and May seem to have been happy. The child was spotted on a chalk down in Wiltshire with a carrion crow on her shoulder and a beatific smile on her face. And in Somerset, rolling round in the River Parrett at Langport with a couple of porpoises that had come upriver with the rising tide, and bowing to the applauding audience on the bridge when she crawled ashore up the mud. And offering wood sorrel to a party of schoolchildren who filed past her in the wood where she had slept. And singing among, and apparently to, the gorse on Exmoor. And snatching fistfuls of Cornish surf and throwing them in her own face. And lying on her front from first to last light, watching the foraging and march of ants, and trying to name individual ants, and learning the schedule of a lizard, and then, when the moon took over from the sun, calling down the tawny owl whose eyes were the same colour as hers. And though there was no one to see just what happened, fox prints led straight up to where the child had passed the night, and there were marks in the sand and the grass of what looked like tumbling.

But in June there was a new and darker tone to the reports. The child was seen in Dorset, trying to revive a fossil ammonite and then reburying it on the beach before moving off to throw beached starfish back into the sea.

A Hampshire pig farmer was disconcerted by the sight of a child who watched from the road as the pigs were loaded on to a lorry, and then tried to unbolt the gates to the long hangars where the pigs were raised. When the police arrived the child was nowhere to be seen.

There was a tailback and lots of hooting in a small Sussex lane because a child was walking along, scraping dead animals off the tarmac and placing them reverently on the verge.

The tenant of a huge cereal farm in Cambridgeshire didn't know whether to be outraged or amused when, from his air-conditioned tractor, he saw a child throwing wildflower seed into a hundred-acre field of wheat, but his neighbour's wife cried – she wasn't sure why – when the child crossed the farm-yard carrying a bag full of fresh grass to give to the cattle that never left the indoor fattening facility.

The police just tut-tutted when they heard about electric fences being pulled down, but took more seriously an epidemic of slashed tyres at an abattoir. They picked up the child, who was repatriating roadkill on a motorway, but there was never anything solid to link her to the tyres, so they dropped her in Cambridge city centre, with advice to get home, get a job and get a life.

In Cambridge, several correspondents had seen her looking mesmerically into butchers' shops and courting the wary pigeons in the market square.

But there (unless we speculate unfairly about some unusual burglaries and acts of vandalism in eastern and southern England) the trail goes cold until, one cold autumn night, the child, emaciated, filthy and tearful, knocked on the door of the community café and asked if she could come back.

The manager was torn. The child had been trouble. He could do without that sort of trouble again. But, though he'd been exculpated by the inquiry, the child's departure hadn't been good for his or the centre's reputation. This was a chance for redemption. Since the child had returned, plainly she harboured no grudge. Here she was, accepting responsibility for her defection – or at least that's how it would be seen.

What did the child want now? he asked. She was clear. A job in the back room, where she couldn't see the sky, and a bedroom, ideally noisy and shared with lots of others, from which, again, the sky was invisible.

The manager looked quizzically at the child. Strange requests, certainly. Some mental health issues, no doubt. But nothing to worry about. Perhaps the child was just lonely (hence the request for a rumbustious dormitory) and rather agoraphobic (hence the fear of the sky). Nothing they couldn't deal with. And besides, they needed someone to chop and wash: no one else wanted to do that.

So yes, he said benevolently. Welcome home. Room fourteen. Here's a key.

That was forty years ago. The child, now white-haired, stooped and twisted, is a fixture in the café, which has gone through several rebrandings. She sleeps still in room fourteen, still chops and washes silently in the back room, and seldom looks up from her chopping board. She has not been outside since she came back that autumn night, except for fire alarms, when she potters outside and looks determinedly at her feet until she's told she can return.

MAYFLY

Numerous species

A female mayfly, impregnated a minute earlier, crashed on to the surface of a Scottish river that had sprung high up on a mountain where red deer waded through heather and eagles rode the spirals of hot air.

Water wicked up her wings. In a moment she was soggy. She would never fly again, but her instinct for the air – though she had known the air in her present form for only an hour, and in her earlier form only for a day – made her flail her new wings.

The flailings sent rings across the river and thrills of pressure into a stripe of nerve down the side of a speckled brown trout. The trout swam towards the centre of the rings, which meant that he rose through the river into the shadow of an overhanging birch, the pressure making his flanks scream louder and louder. Now he saw the mayfly, her body lashing the river film and squeezing, desperately squeezing. She could not know the trout was coming. It had been just over a day since she last had eyes that could see under water.

The skin of the river tore, and the mayfly was dragged through the tear into the mouth of the fish. But in the last spasm before she died her fertilized eggs squirted from her body and sank down to the stones on the riverbed. All but one were eaten. The embryo – already a male – rolled beneath a piece of gravel, and a new story started.

No: that's not right. This story, like all other stories, did not start at any point that we can see, or indeed at any *point* in either time or space, because it started before starts; before time and space were forged into the forms from which we imagine our homes to be built.

Even as the embryo sank through the layers of the river, the cosmos inside it swirled, condensed and crystallized. It had its own tides and currents: tides of cells and currents of enzymes. Islands would soon rise. A misty archipelago would focus into legs, feet, and mandibles like scythe blades.

A crayfish grazed across the stream bed, sweeping with its chopstick arms to turn the gravel, gathering embryos. The embryos clanked down between the hard plates of its jaws. It was an invader from North America, went the rhetoric of the agencies who warred against it; an alien who would disturb the delicate equipoise of the mountain. The posters did not mention that the worthy biologists behind the posters were invaders themselves.

The crayfish saw the rounded edge of the embryo, clear against the craggy edges of the gravel. There was no *thought* in its brain, deep under its chitin helmet, of its own reproductive destiny, but the equations said that, as a matter of thermodynamic fact, the embryo would give the final shove to a chemical reaction which would flush into the stream a new dynasty of snapping, chomping crayfish.

Its mouth was open. Its pincers closed round the embryo. But its excitement had caught the attention of a big yellow eye with a black pupil – an eye attached, by a complex arrangement of bone and horn, to a dagger wielded by a long speckled neck. The neck uncoiled, the dagger plunged, and the crayfish was broken and minced by the heron and there would be no new crayfish dynasty that year.

So the tides and the currents in the embryo continued to flow. The islands knotted, knitted, grappled, sharpened and smoothed.

There were knees, spikes, and bearings; oiled hinges, sheltered valleys for telegraph wires and pits for racks of sensors.

It was not only a change of shape. The thing got bigger and more obviously male. Cells divided, and the divided cells divided, and the thing swelled. Somewhere in the thing, or in the river, or in the way that things were, was a blueprint which said not only how many knees should be built, and how deep the pits should be, but when each bit of swelling should stop. What was this thing under the gravel? It was a device for eating, growing, changing and continuing; much more but not less than a machine; a tapered, three-tailed, scimitar-jawed tank. Fishermen, presumably to mock his ugliness, called him a nymph.

The cell-swirling and streaming accelerated: think of complex roundabouts, over- and underpasses, motorways with disciplined lanes, filamentous side-roads, all at rush hour. The traffic was powered by algae rasped from the rocks; algae that had solidified the summer sun, making it chewable. The nymph's feathery gills fluttered on the sides of his abdomen. He would have needed them in less vibrant water than this, but the river bubbled down fast from the high tops, filling the water with oxygen, and the nymph could get through his armour-plating the oxygen needed to burn the algae and power his engines.

Though it would be a year before they were used, already sperm were being assembled; their heads sharpening and hardening, preparing to drill through an egg membrane next summer; their tails flexing, ready for the race and the push.

Trout, fat on mayfly bodies, cruised through the only sky the nymph would know, and were themselves hunted through the sky by men who threw them fake mayflies made from hare fur and partridge feathers and tied on nylon extruded from a nozzle in Belarus. When the trout were deceived the men were happy – not because they needed the food (they needed much less food, not more), but because it seemed to them that they were being the sort of creatures they were meant to be, which seldom happens to humans. One Londoner never clubbed his trout, but left them flapping and gasping in the grass. 'I will flap and gasp and die one day,' he said to himself. 'The more I see and study it now, the better it will be for me when that day comes.'

There were great dangers for the nymph. It was almost certain that he would not survive, which is the case for almost all young things in the world, and all his efforts sought to confound that near certainty. His future was a statistical nonsense, populated by epic horrors: carnivorous worms with the jaws of a kitchen blender; fish with the teeth of a wolverine. When rain swept in from the sea, thrashing the uplands and making the deer cower in the woods, the nymph lived for days in a rock storm which might have ground him as a peppercorn, shielded from the worst by a deer's jaw wedged in the riverbed.

A nearby dipper – a little bobbity white-aproned bird which flew under water – specialized in nymphs. It had several launch pads along the stream – rocks overlooking its flight paths and killing fields – each white with droppings made from the bodies of *processes*; made, like all meat, of frustrated potential turned into actual but different potential.

The nymph escaped all the horrors. This was not skill, but luck, aided and abetted by a tendency to stay in the shadows, and a healthy portfolio of digestive enzymes.

The sun went south, and who can blame it. A stag, shot on the scree below the summit, tumbled dead to the water. The stalker gralloched him there and slung his entrails into the stream before dragging him to the game larder in the big house.

The entrails seeded a new generation of algae downstream, and the nymph galloped through his next six iterations, the sperm, the legs and the wings creeping ever closer to those mysterious working drawings, wherever they were to be found.

He would moult twenty-three times in all before next summer, casting off his coat to let the adult he was brewing have more room to stretch and form. He was not that adult. The adult legs folded inside him were no use to him. He was a factory and a warehouse for the legs.

~

The stream cooled. The factory shut down. Its chemical reactions could not work until the sun returned, and the nymph now just stored his successor. With the last of the sun he crawled under a stone and stayed there. It makes no sense to say that he slept, for there was no processing of his experience; no consolidation or cognitive stocktaking. It is better to say that he endured, paralysed and suspended by the cold; encysted without becoming a cyst. He would barely have squirmed if a fish had chewed him.

The land had changed already. The red deer were not red. The rime that whitened their coats thinned but did not vanish during the day. Their breath froze and fell as clouds of ice crystals. The breath smelt of pear drops, for the deer were starving and burning their own muscle. The ravens had crusted brown heads from rummaging inside the bodies of dead deer. The estate cancelled the hind-stalking for the year: cold would do the culling the rifles usually did. The voles lived in a labyrinth of snow tunnels. The owls' breastbones cut through their skin. The eagles moved to the valley.

The river's pelt thickened and hardened, first to leather and then to glass. Wildcats walked across it on the way to kill the farm chickens left by the foxes and pine martens. The river's life shrank to the bottom. It was good in these times to be cold-blooded like a fish, and untyrannized by a thermostat; not forced into the deadly open by the appetite of a metabolic motor.

It is a strange thing that when the cold is most vicious the sun is already well on its way back. The Earth had wobbled round its poles, and this part of Scotland was hurtling through space towards the fire. A raven (or, rather, a structure buried deep in the raven's head) was the first to notice. The structure was a vigilant clock, ticking silently through the dark of the winter and the dark of the skull, fed cues by the raven's eyes, timing the creep of sunrise and sunset and, via various biochemical flunkies, issuing demands to the genitals: blood flow up: mitosis and meiosis on. And to the throat: time for the laryngeal flex and stretch to undo the winter sloth. And to the psyche: from the blasted birch to the otter's rock to the tall oak to the fence is yours and none but yours. So declare it.

In the nymph's body, too, chemical reactions had started to cycle. They sped up, and potent substances sprayed from their wheels into the cells of wings and legs. The two one-use penises, one for each of the female's openings, distended and braced. As the spring gathered and the last of the ice gave in and the deer returned to the high tops and the birds fluffed and threatened, the nymph shrugged off more of his coats. Soon he would shrug off the river itself, and the dimensions in which his form now compelled him to crawl. Did he *aspire* to the air and the sun and genetic immortality? I don't know what that word means here. He certainly tried hard to avoid missing the chance of the air. He filled himself with organisms that would one day power the blast-off. He faced off the small fish that would have reassembled his components into their bodies. When the dipper grabbed one of his legs, he span so fast around his own shoulder that his leg came off and he was flushed downstream to safety. His skin split not only because the physics governing the behaviour of its component material said that the molecules along the seams should separate, but because he wriggled. And he need not have wriggled, or at least not when he did. He suppressed his wriggling when squadrons of fish appeared in his sky.

His body was being parasitized. Another body, quite different from his, fed on it, sucking nutrients into structures that he, himself, the embodied thing that he was, would never use. Lying next to him, inside his own skin, cluttering up his space, making his cuticle like a village hall hosting a jumble sale, were legs, wings and reproductive organs as useless to him as an umbrella. He slaved and risked all for them.

Humans came out with the sun: walkers who strode up the path, walking not through the landscape at all, but through a map; brushing not bracken but coordinates; with a goal in mind that was not the summit of the mountain, but a point on a GPS. Since not even the bracken really existed for them, it's not surprising that the riverbed didn't exist at all.

But there were children too, who, in the brief moment before they were digitized, came with jam jars, and nets made of their mothers' old tights, and a capacity for surprise, and were changed by the gravel between their toes and the eyes of the carrion crows who came to watch them and who remembered their faces from last year.

The nymph was scooped into a palm sticky with wine gums

and whooped at until he nearly dried out, and his hairy cyborg legs were peered at through a magnifying glass which almost set him on fire, and then he was placed tenderly into the deadliest place in the river – but it was all right in the end.

The fish were well awake now, and eggs were hardening inside the dipper, making her hungry and busy. The sun, like the crayfish, crawled under the rocks where the nymph hid. There was no life without the sun, but there was also no death without it.

The nymph dodged the jaws, got faster at burying himself, and took to browsing at night.

April came. He had moulted nineteen times. Inside he was tender. The river crunched as nymphs were caught and recycled. Where they were eaten by adult trout or crayfish, that seemed unfair, for the mangled joints and organs were new and complex, and they added only a fraction to the length of an already complete fish, and didn't greatly increase the fish's chance of reproduction. Where nymphs were eaten by burgeoning juveniles it was easier to see God's point: it didn't seem quite so wanton and wasteful.

The nymph was running out of chances now. Every time a nymph was caught, he became more vulnerable. He had hidden in a herd, and the herd had thinned. Then, with just six weeks of refinement left, respite came. Two thousand miles away, over a dark pit full of sea monsters, air started to coil. It made a black pot which pulled salt water and terrified fish up into itself. It moved east, snorting as it approached Ireland. It sank a fishing boat and dismembered her crew on the rocks of Donegal, decapitated a supermarket in Derry, exposed as fraudulent the marketing blurb of some bungalow-builders on Lewis, and spent its last strength and dropped its last fish and water on the mountain. The river rose six inches in an hour, and four feet in twelve, washing worms, slugs, earwigs and centipedes out of the soil and on towards the sea. With such a flesh-fest swishing round their heads the trout forgot about nymphs, and couldn't have seen them anyway for all the mud. Boys from the village, dressed in thrilling camouflage, slunk upriver at twilight, dangled worms into the deep pools and hauled out bloated trout still full of worm-meat.

The mud lasted longer than the worms. By the time the river ran clear the nymph was on his twenty-third and final moult. His sperm were mature. His eyes, which had been lustrous, were misty. His mouth-parts, previously cavernous and spiky with stalactites, were barely visible; his gut, formerly a barrage balloon, was now an empty condom; and his feathery gills had been plucked. The wings of the next stage, the sub-imago, were folded inside a packet like a camping chair in a drawstring bag.

Around him the surviving nymphs, most of whom he'd never met, were preparing to launch and unfold. They had been conceived at about the same time and shared the same river, but had different joys, feeds and stresses – yet, male and female, they would burst into the upper world together. If they did not, they would not reproduce.

How did they coordinate the launch? There are speculations about day length, positive feedback loops and chemical signalling. They raise many questions, provide few fundamental answers, and, though reassuring if you're queasy about invoking new mechanisms, involve ludicrously improbable chains of causation. Far better and more scientific to say for now: 'No idea. It's a mystery.' But the nymphs *seem* connected by some sort of weird field, for they turn up to the light and the air as iron filings order themselves under the charisma of a magnet.

They moved out from under their rocks, their favourite pieces of gravel, and their own weedy bailiwicks, and their new opaque eyes swivelled towards the sun. They heaved to squeeze gas, extracted from the peat water, into the space between the cuticles and the new sub-imago's body. The gas prised away the old cuticles so that when the nymphs reached the surface the sub-imagos would explode into the sun, unencumbered by past lives. The gas was also a buoyancy device. Until now, the nymphs' food had been at the bottom of the stream. Floating would have been deadly, for it would have meant hanging in the flight paths of fish. But not to change radically is to die. Old bodies and old dimensions had to be sloughed off. Now, trailing a stream of bubbles, the nymphs rose on their last journey; the sub-imagos on their first.

Once a decision is made, the natural world honours speed and punishes dithering. Our nymph – now our sub-imago – had squeezed well, the buoyancy jacket was full, and he accelerated up. He hit the surface, which was as solid with sticky molecular forces as a barn door. He lay for a moment, which might have been fatal, in the no-man's land between river and sky, nailed to the water with electrostatic tacks, but tugged to the sky by fear so rudimentary that it was barely fear at all, and by instinct so sophisticated that it looked like the most arcane magic.

There is often thrashing when an organism passes from one plane to another; thrashing under the paws of a leopard, in the beak of a bee-eater, or on a hospital bed. But rarely is the thrashing as important for the transition as it is here. Here it snapped the last glutinous strands connecting the old to the new, forced brake fluid into his stiffening wings and shocked his legs into trembling attention. His legs and tails had been telescoped tightly inside him. Now, in the flurry, the telescopes were extended: his leg tarsi extruded to twice their larval length, his tail to three times its larval length. The water now had a lot more to grasp – and that was dangerous.

The water had had the nymph for a year. It would not easily let him go; and it had several advantages as it tussled with the air for dominion. During the struggle, the sub-imago's new legs were held stiffly under his body, ready to push off from the water's surface as from a diving board. That meant they were entangled in the electrical thicket of the water. When at last the cuticle fell away and he rested briefly, the heavy hot air surging into his respiratory tubes, his hind and middle legs and much of his abdomen were on the water too. And when the oxygen in that air, oxygen breathed out by heather and birch, had ignited the engines for blast-off, the first flailing downstrokes of the sub-imaginal wings beat against the stream.

But this fight against the water was precisely the fight for which the sub-imago had evolved since the Carboniferous. He had poured immense resources of energy and materials into the battle. The sole purpose of the conflict was to lift his penis and sperm out of the water. He did not have to be a good flyer to do that, and indeed he was nothing like as good a flyer as the adult whose genitalia and gametes he bore. If he won the battle, he would die in a few hours. To win he needed a water-repellent body, legs and wings – achieved by a dense covering of tiny hairs. As an adult he would be bald and glossy. He would meet water only when he died, and hairs then would be pointless.

This drama of chemistry and engineering was played out on a bend in the river, where alders reached far out over the water, heather ejaculated its pollen into the wind from the sea, and otters sometimes played. A ptarmigan feather, torn out by a peregrine, drifted through the pool bearing a cargo of lice, and a big old trout, drunk and lazy on insect bodies, sucked in the feather to join the paste of newborn limbs and wings in his stomach.

The trout rose again.

The sub-imago had a moment to shake off his cuticle. One final heave of his abdomen expelled the last of the gas from his bowels. He winched his knees under him to the take-off position. They nearly split.

His head stretched towards the sun, pulling his thorax free of the river. The trout was circling; there was no time for a trial run. The sub-imago's tumescent wings traced eleven figures of eight, his knees unfolded, his foot hinges opened, his abdomen lifted, his legs detonated.

It was not enough. His wings slapped the water.

But the feather in the trout's belly and so the ptarmigan and the peregrine and the ptarmigan's ancestors and possibly the lice and certainly the breeze off the alder that had put the feather over the trout's head, and so the thrust of the eagle's wing that had caused an eddy in the breeze, and the blowing of a minke whale in the Sound that, folded into a cloud, had dripped on to the alder the month before, and the fart of a Korean reefer ship, and the hydrogen sulphide from a rotting pterodactyl, and the spin of an electron in the blazing heart of Alpha Centauri – saved the insect. For the fish was disgusted by the feather, and rose to spit it beside the sub-imago. The moment of spitting was the moment of salvation. For as he spat it out, the trout saw a less hairy, waterlogged female nearby. He took it instead of our sub-imago.

Our sub-imago's hairs shoved the water aside. His wings peeled away from the river, made another eleven figures of eight, and he rose falteringly into a new world. His sub-imaginal legs had been made for this one explosion.

He dropped on to a leaf of the alder which was already crowded with sub-imagos. The tree was busy with tiny olive birds with artery-forcep beaks, all labouring for young who screeched with straining necks for food. In two months' time the fledglings would fly across seas and a great desert, or die.

A peck shook the leaf. The mayfly lost its grip and swung off, holding on only with one leg. Had he fallen, it would have been the end. But one leg was enough. The chiffchaff did not see the leg, and moved on. An eddy from the tail of the departing bird twisted the leaf for a moment, and in the last of the light the mayfly clambered on to the leaf to start the night's work.

His wings were now redundant. They were crude, bristly and clumsy, designed just for that one four-foot journey. As the owl's claws met in the body of a mouse at the foot of the alder, the smooth adult wings, already formed in the nymph, split their constraining packets, spread and tensed. As the otter cracked a crayfish in the alder pool, spilling mayfly larvae on to her tongue, our mayfly's adult legs, which had been concertinaed inside the sub-imago's legs, unfolded down and out, cracking the shells of his old legs and trebling in length, acquiring spindly grabbing tarsi for grasping the female. His tail doubled in length, the better to steer in the wind of the coming day. His tiny, pointless mouth-parts and gills shrank to nothing. His wings, legs and tail hardened in the moonlight. His midgut, useless for feeding, now filled with air to keep him aloft as he inseminated, and his abdomen was as tense as a waistcoated clubman's after steak and kidney pudding. The females' eggs had been ready at the sub-imaginal stage. In mayflies, as in humans, the females waited tetchily for the males to catch up.

The first and last sun the adults would ever know climbed out of the sea. The birds rose with it. By ten, when the sun came round to our mayfly's side of the alder, a quarter of the adult mayflies had been eaten. By two, half of them were dead. By six, only a fifth survived. And this was their moment.

The males made the first move, launching from the alder on their one-use legs into the fitful breeze down the glen. It took them to a wide arc in the river with a gravel beach, a dark pool where the big salmon lay, safe from artificial flies because a birch rampart guarded the river, making casting impossible, and safe indeed from all humans but the most stealthy and amphibious child with a gaff.

There our mayfly, in a cloud of ten thousand other survivors, began to dance, bouncing up and down in the haze, burning off the last of his fuel, spraying pheromones that drifted back to the females, who now pushed off into the air themselves for the first and last time, and were caught by the breeze and furled into the dance. The silent frenzy doubled. The breath of a drinking stag moved the dance further downstream. A raven, gliding to the corpse of a fox cub, split the dancers into four. A merlin with its claws in the back of a grey wagtail split them again. The wake from a rowdy platoon of mallard ruffled the water and engulfed a few. Trout leaped clear of the river and trawled open-mouthed through the ballroom.

Were there too many bodies for real choice? Would mating happen just with the dancer opposite, whoever he or she happened to be? No: their degree of resolution was far higher than ours: the individuation massive, the pheromones as different as Chanel No. 5 and Coco Mademoiselle, the power of the wings and the curve of the penises as distinct as a Christian Dior suit.

Our mayfly's tank was running dry. He could not keep up

the dance for long. He felt himself sinking. He tried, between bounces, to force more air into his gut, but it was full. A few more yo-yo-ings and he would be spent. Now! Now! Everything to allure, to flash the light from his wings into her eyes, to brandish his genitals, to flood her olfactory pits with his signals and flush out his competitors' molecules.

Yes! A demure, quiet-living female, hatched in the safest of pools, kept trout-free by an otter holt, twitched her abdomen. He rose from below her, moved behind her; clutched her to himself. They rose together, he shuddered, and then he fell away, empty, done, finished, over. He did not try to stay above the water now. There would be no second chance. He had no energy even to struggle. A trout took him.

His mate was not long behind him. Three minutes and twenty seconds, to be precise. Her transition to adulthood had been less arduous than his. She did not have to build and extrude such long legs or make the running on the dance floor. But she had to carry and deposit a bomb bay of eggs.

There was little real choice about where to drop them. Her own engines were shutting down. She landed by a raft of birch twigs, milked out the fertilized eggs, lost whatever consciousness she had had, and was broken in a tug of war between two sticklebacks. The eggs sank. Their chromosomal spindles started to spin.

They hummed, wove and spliced. Templates were fashioned; base pairs slotted neatly into their places; a complex mesh of electronic bonds crept across each egg, snaring roving molecules and building them into the matrix. Atomic trains shuttled materials; shunting yards organized them; pulleys hoisted loads. Soon there would be shadowy legs and fuzzy jaws, and then nymphs would step out of the shadow.

The conditions were perfect. The water was clean. The eggs were tucked invisibly under the gravel, and unlikely to be swept far in a spate. The otters had decimated the crayfish. Yet by the start of July it was clear that all was not well. The trains sputtered; there had been a derailment in the shunting yard. There embryos were foggy; no limbs or teeth could be seen in the fog.

There was a farm upstream, a troubled place, owned by a disillusioned refugee from Essex who, cold-shouldered by the local farmers, the hill and his bank manager, picked up some bad habits and a bottle of whisky a day. There was talk in the village about sheep being dipped in the river, run-off from the sprayed bracken, and about the pipe draining slurry from his cows. It is hard to know what to believe.

Next summer, for the first time since the end of the last Ice Age, there were no mayflies on the river, and the dipper starved.

This is how most stories are: glory, glory, glory, and a sudden end with an inconclusive cause.

RABBIT

Oryctolagus cuniculus

It started with a rape in a wet wood, one raw bitter February night. With a grab of the neck in the teeth, a straddling, a pointless scream, and then blood on the soil.

Against the odds, the pregnancy stuck inside the thin, hope-less, lower-caste mother. She swelled, her bones drained into the foetal bones and, four weeks later, O,* along with three others, was squeezed from the hot wet dark of the womb into the cold dry dark of a hole under a bramble bush. She found a nipple and pushed her sisters off.

For another three weeks the mother came to her at night, scratching away the earth that plugged the hole where O lay, and every night O drained a bit more from her mother. By the time that O could feed herself, her siblings were dead, and their mother, dry and crackling like paper, could die too. She died underground. O nudged the body, pulled at the empty teat, and next morning crawled up the tunnel to meet the day. She pushed through the soil, more like a mole than a rabbit, and the ground squeezed her out as her mother had done. It was more of a birth than the first one.

Her eyes had been open since her seventh day, but they had had nothing to do down there in the ground. Now she shook the earth off her head, blinked, and the world crashed into her. Light gushed, grass towered. Everything moved all the time. Her new

---

* For *Oryctolagus cuniculus*.

eyes followed the play of sun and shadow, the march of armoured bugs, the trembling of stems and rocking of trunks, the flickering of wings, the sedate glides and febrile flappings.

In the earth things had been simple. It was just her and a nipple. Now there was suddenly more to consider. Here there were many things. Down there it was just instinct: drink, sleep, stretch. Here there were options. This field quivered not just with shadow and heartbeat, but with personhood. There were new smells in the field, and far stronger than the cow dung, the fox and the diesel was the smell of *purpose*. Everything smelt of it. It drove those martial legs and rasping tongues, drew the stems out into the void, and made wings turn that way rather than this. All non-humans and few humans have the smell of the purpose of others in their nostrils all the time.

O had it in her nose for a hundred wondering, panting breaths. And then she rose above the grass, the field, the cows, and the barren blackthorn hedges. The scrape where she had been born – which until a moment before had been the universe – became a dot, and then she floated past a wood, and the universe was lost.

The trees and hedges had had height: lots of it. But now, as she looked down, they had lost their height completely, and were patches and lines. Far below she saw the roof of a farm, and wondered what the roof would do next. A thin grey snake (humans knew it as a river) slithered from the farm and met another thin grey snake, and she could not wrench her eyes from them. On the snakes shining things crawled up and down. She thought they must be fleas like the ones that sometimes crept over her face, and scratched herself in sympathy. On one side the wind bit her; on the other the sun was thin.

Ahead, a long way off, a claw stuck into a shiningness, and there was wool round the claw. The claw was a crescent of land slicing into the sea, and the wool was the mist driving in from Wales. Closer, a tongue licked at nothing, and this, though she was never to meet or know it, was the flag on a Norman church.

There were more shiningnesses: shining snakes winding to the sea, and big patches of shining. Once, when she came close to one of the patches, she saw a darker patch running across it at the same pace and in the same direction as she was running through the air, and though she was to meet her own shadow again, she never met it again on a lake like this.

She came still closer to the shining patch. Like the fur on her own back, it was stirred by the wind. But in a smoother piece unstroked by the wind she saw a big bird (though she did not know it was a bird) rising towards her, holding a small bundle with long ears, and the bundle looked back at her before dropping back again towards the lake. Later she would see her own nose reflected in a puddle and would understand.

At the edge of the shiningness was a small bent tree which moved. It had a long branch which whipped the water, and it turned small eyes up to O, and shouted (O did not know it was a shout, though she would know that later), and O swung away and climbed, and never again met or knew a fisherman or a road.

O's eyes could look almost all around her. Above her she saw an inviting nest of dappled feathers. Legs sprouted from the nest, and the feet at the end of the legs gripped O. Behind her was a tilting fan of barred brown, and up ahead was a hook. To each side was a narrow brown roof. But it wasn't much of a roof, for it didn't stretch far on either side, and didn't give much shelter, and sometimes it flapped up and down.

O tried to twist, as she had done in the ground, but she was pricked in eight places, and she screeched, and was pricked more. Usually the buzzard gripped hard when he grabbed a rabbit from the ground, and squeezed so that his eight knives met in the liver and the spleen and the bowels, and that was an end of it. That made for an easier journey back to the treetop platform where he preferred to eat. But this rabbit didn't struggle. Why should she? This flight, for her, was like the sucking and the sleeping. It was how things were. Her mother's teeth had sometimes drawn blood from her neck as she picked up the kits to rearrange them in the tunnel. The buzzard's talons weren't much different. But now, as she squirmed, a point burst through the skin and stopped just short of a kidney. That wasn't like her mother's nip. Her natural opiates surged through her, as if someone had injected heroin, and her eyes fluttered and shut, and her body drooped, and the buzzard thought the job was done.

For generations the buzzard's family had eaten by choice on a tall beech. Sometimes they couldn't. A really big rabbit couldn't be lifted, and had to be carved and eaten on the ground. But if he could it was better to eat where his parents had taught him, watching between mouthfuls the road, the goat farm, the church and the sea.

He was going to the beech now, taking care, for in this wind even this small rabbit made steering tricky.

Two crows, young, clever, subtle and ambitious, but with old minds, were pecking fitfully at a pheasant at the roadside. They saw the buzzard. Feud and fun were more important than food, and they took off to intercept him. They had a well-practised drill. One flew at his face. He stalled. The other went for his tail. The buzzard twisted round, slashed with his beak, missed, rearranged himself on his flight path, shrugged off another feint, saw the beech ahead, and began his glide down.

The crows weren't finished. They did the same again: one to the front, one to the back. The buzzard, outraged at the insolence, and remembering the dignity of his ancestors but not the rabbit in his claws, lashed out with his feet. O tumbled down, still unconscious. She was jolted awake as she fell into a natural basket of springing saplings at the top of an old willow. There she crouched, listening to the squabble of birds, the muttering of the tree, the gibbering of a tractor, and bells begging people to leave their laptops and come to worship.

For hours she could not move: she was frozen by merciful paralysis. So the crows, which had seen her drop, but not seen her land, stalked vainly round the tree, barging through the nettles and tilting their heads to look under logs. They soon gave up, and went back to the pheasant, leaving O alone with the muttering, the gibbering and the bells.

She lay there all day, not wondering if this was the end, for she knew only about beginnings, and because there were no lines in the world she knew. You need lines for endings.

The sun, never really having got started, handed over to sea-drizzle and gloom in the mid-afternoon. Cows sauntered along the lanes to be milked a second time. Jackdaws clinked like struck cups. A thing like the fisherman slung a chain round a tree stump, shackled it to the tractor and hauled up a community that had been gestating there since Drake routed the Armada, gaining complexity as humans had haemorrhaged complexity, learning new ways of cooperation and community while humans perfected loneliness and selfishness. The stump and its inhabitants were driven away and slung on a tip full of fridges and microwaves. Anger at this might have kept O warm, but she did not understand, and shivered.

A tawny owl in the nearby copse opened one eye, then the other, unfolded, shook, stretched and flew over towards the willow, hoping for a vole in the rough grass. He banked next to O's basket, saw something odd, swivelled his head, saw a little rabbit on a tree top, choked, squawked, and flustered off to somewhere normal. Owls are conservative birds. They don't like change. They're fond of their presumptions. A meal in the wrong place is not a windfall but an offence against all that is sacred.

The owl's big alarmed eyes and stubby tongue scared O out of her torpor. She scrabbled and scrambled and found that she had big back legs with explosive muscle, and the muscles exploded and O shot up and out of the basket and tumbled again, bouncing off the willow stems into the nettles where the crows had hunted for her that morning.

~

Before sunrise the next day, O's father, king of an old rabbit citadel deep in a tangled bank, swaggered from hole to hole. Lesser bucks edged out of his way as he grazed threateningly towards them. Some of the bigger males, perhaps with a view to the crown, stood their ground for a while, but fled when he ran towards them. The king's chin was hairless, for he rubbed it everywhere, leaving scent from his chin glands saying: 'This is mine.' Other males had crusty yellow beards of shame that announced that they had no place of their own – no place to wipe their chins – but were craven courtiers.

The swagger stopped as the king approached his queen. His sperm weren't hers alone – he'd empty himself into any female on heat – but his affection and loyalty were. He came to her each time as a bashful suitor, timorous and scared of rejection.

He needn't have worried that morning. The queen basked on her side in the moonlight, languid, as on a brocaded divan, her belly open to him. He inched alongside. He nibbled her neck. She didn't object, but to show him that he needed her more than she needed him she didn't respond. He licked her forehead. She didn't respond. He licked her ears, now feeling slighted. She didn't respond. Affronted and insecure, he went off to bully some young bucks to make him feel better about himself, and to show the others (who had been watching the coquettish queen shrewdly, wondering what it meant for the byzantine politics of the court) that he was still very much in charge. He wound menacingly towards a would-be challenger, his hindquarters raised to make his back legs look bigger. The challenger didn't move, and the king leaped on him, ripping a mouthful of fur and skin from his throat and wiping his chin all over the upstart's face until he was blind with the king's hormones. For a while, wherever the challenger went, he'd declare by the stink of his face the sovereignty of the king.

The other rabbits were relieved. They liked to know where they stood. This had been a long, stern monarchy, and they were glad that they needn't renegotiate their alliances yet.

Normal social life was exhausting, but social and political uncertainty were more exhausting still.

~

There was not much social or political complexity in Ken's life, and there was no negotiation.

Like O, he'd been conceived by a rape in that wood, or so his mother said. Perhaps his resentment of that conception, and the life that followed, explained what he did to the wood.

As a child he skipped school and went to the wood instead. If it was hot he took a magnifying glass and boiled ants in their own juice. If it was cold he took tweezers and pulled off their legs on one side, so that they limped in circles. He placed them carefully, so that together they traced the demonic patterns he'd dreamed up in his bedroom. He pinned live beetles to boards, and trimmed minnow tails with scissors and watched them swim and gasp in a glass of Irn-Bru. He lit a nest of black-bird nestlings with lighter fluid stolen from the corner shop, crucified a broken-winged thrush, and played football with a hedgehog.

As he got older he acquired a taste for less immediate pleasures. He ripped away the bark at the feet of a clump of fir trees, and thrilled over the months as they drooped, drowned and died. He did the same for all the trees of a rookery, and four years later the rooks were homeless. In the spring he lapped up the silence. He shoved barbed wire down the gates of a badger sett, and was pleased to see the work the badgers had to put in to dig round it.

In the chicken factory where he worked he was known as an excellent worker: disciplined, focused and committed. The workers there didn't stay long. The pay was poor, the hours long and the work monotonous. But Ken was never bored. He was always eager, rejoicing in the rolling eyes of the birds going round on the line, hanging by their feet. Sometimes he'd snip off a toe or two with the pliers that were always in his pocket. Sometimes he'd turn down the voltage on the stunner so that the birds went live into the scalding tank, and get a bonus that week for detecting the fault.

Today was a Sunday; one of Ken's rare days off. He woke, alone as ever, to radio ads for fitted kitchens and hot tubs, ate a slice of last night's pizza from the box in front of the TV, and went out to the back yard. He opened the door of a hutch, reached in, pulled out two drooping fur cylinders and dropped them into a wooden box. Hoisting the box on to his shoulder by its carrying strap, he left the house, dumped the box in the back of the old car which stood outside, put on the camouflage jacket that lay on the passenger seat and drove off in the dark.

The wood was twenty minutes away. He drove fast, lips squeezed hard together, eyes boring along the beam of the headlamps. That, he supposed, was how soldiers drove on their way to the front. He was planning the campaign. He'd been planning it for a while.

He parked on the roadside, took out the box, a bag and a stick, climbed a gate, and made his way along the hedge and into the wood. As he reached the warren the sun was starting to climb. The rabbits, hearing and smelling him, stamped their feet, scrunched their noses and lolloped below ground.

Ken knew the warren well – he had a map of the labyrinth up on a pinboard by his bed – and now, having dumped the box and the stick at the foot of the bank, he pegged nets around all the holes, making escape unlikely. Next he dived into the box and took out one of the two drooping things. They were ferrets. He hadn't fed them for three days so that they'd be hungry and keen. All the droop had gone from this one. It slithered between his hands like a white steel spring. Its eyes bulged red, as if its head were tense with blood. He pinched it between its toes to make it bitter. It sank its teeth into his finger. He smiled, prised the teeth out, put on a collar with a radio transmitter, tuned the transmitter to a receiver which he put in his pocket, and put the ferret down at the entrance to one of the holes. It swayed for a moment like a leech on a leaf, scenting, and then oscillated underground.

The king sat in his throne-room, deep in the hill. Here he held court, slept, ate his faeces to wring the last nutrients from the grass, and canoodled with his queen. Usually he'd have his nose towards the web of tunnels that led to the room from outside, so that he could receive the obeisance of supplicants and defendants. But now, along with his queen, he had his face to the wall, ready to kick an intruder. For the stink of fear filled the tunnels. This was the hot musk of weasel – an ancient enemy – but with a patina of chips, newsprint, diesel and deodorant; more fearsome because of its impurity.

The king heard the sounds of panic: stamping, mewing, stampeding, and the swish of his own blood in his neck and ears. Those who say that non-humans have no sense of self have never seen – really seen – an animal quivering because the self (whatever that is) might be snuffed out or relocated.

It had not come to that for the king. He was confident that his back legs could stun or disembowel any contaminated weasel that seeped along his tunnels. His fear was not for his personal body but for his body politic. The boundings and whinings above and around him meant fearsome change.

The queen, normally so aloof and self-possessed, now pushed

close to the king, as if to get inside him, to become him, to make his deadly hindlimbs hers. She wanted to join her self with his so that it was not violated.

The false-weasel-stink was enough for many. They raced from it as if from poison gas.

~

Ken knelt, put his ear to the ground, and heard the panic. It wouldn't be long now. He stood and waited, twirling his stick.

And there was the first! A youngster, blasting from the hole. It saw Ken, skidded as it changed direction, saw the field beyond the wood and freedom from the stink, but did not see the net. Its head went straight through, but its legs wouldn't follow. It was upside down, its face in thistles, when Ken yanked it out, swung it theatrically round his head, and smashed its head on a tree. Ten others followed it into the dark.

~

Still the king and queen waited. The warren was now quiet apart from the sniff and scratch of the approaching fear. The ferret's nose wasn't much use now. There was a strong rabbit smell all around – in their dread many of the rabbits had urinated – and so it was hard to know if any rabbits remained. There was no light at all in most of the tunnels. The only useful senses were hearing and touch. His ears could hear at ten yards breath trickling from the nose of a well-controlled rabbit, and at twenty the stretch of a cramped leg. His body wound round the turns in the tunnels, his skin mapping the walls.

There was something ahead. He knew it, though it was as

still as a live thing can be. He crept forward. He felt the rabbit's heat on his cold nose. When he was on top of the rabbit he'd know very well where to bite. He sprang.

～

Up above, Ken stuck his knife into the rabbits, and their intestines sprang earnestly out as if they'd been frustrated by the constraint of the muscle. He ripped out the bowels and watched as they squirmed in his hand. Then he pushed the guts into the holes – one set for each hole, very systematically, for this was to show them all, rabbits dead and alive, and the wood as a whole, who was in charge. Now he was waiting for the ferret to return. It was taking its time, but this one sometimes did. Perhaps Ken had overdone the starvation, and the ferret had killed and eaten underground, and perhaps even curled up by the corpse to have a sleep after breakfast.

He switched on the ferret-finder. The red light blinked. He held it close to the ground and scanned the bank. At last it bleeped. He moved up the hill. The bleep got louder and more insistent and became a continuous tone. Damn! The devil's own place to dig, if it came to that. The warren was deepest here, and there was an underground rock ledge overhanging the deepest rooms of all. He'd wait a bit, gather up the nets, and hope the ferret came out. He had nothing else to do.

Five cigarettes later he lost patience, picked up the spade and began to dig. The sun was now up and it was hot work. He hung his coat on a tree and mopped his forehead on his shirt. He cursed the fucking idle ferret. He'd teach it all right.

The spade hit stone. He'd reached the overhang. Now what? He probed with a stick and found the edge of the rock. It couldn't be much further now. He drove the spade in again. It went in deep. He heaved out a big load of soil and rubble. The bleep went wild. Nearly there. One more go should do it.

It did. The blade sliced neatly through the ferret's body. The king and queen, who had been cowering behind the ferret, bolted along the tunnel, and were away. Ken turned in time to see that the king had a hole in his left ear – a souvenir of a near miss with a fox.

Ken picked up the two parts of his ferret. They were barely warm. The spade hadn't killed it. The ferret's spring had met the king's kick, which had dislocated the ferret's neck. Ken looked after the fleeing rabbits, fuming. He slung the ferret parts down a rabbit hole, gathered up his gear, strode across the field to the car, and sped off to look at his map of the neighbourhood's rabbit warrens.

~

After her fall into the nettles, O lay still for an hour, watching ants mass round a hoverfly and march it off; watching her own feet, which were new to her and moved in strange ways; watching the hairs, the shadows, and the arches of the plants tilt and shake as the tides of the wind ebbed and flowed; hearing the murmur of roads, the putter-swish, putter-swish of her own heart. Her heart slowed. She began to look around rather than straight ahead. Her neck unfroze. She shook her shoulders, felt empty inside, and nipped off some grass shoots.

She had fed herself! She was away!

But she was an unusual small rabbit. Most very young rabbits, though they are independent very early, have other big and small rabbits around. There are cues to be taken, ruses to be learned, other eyes to watch, other feet to stamp alarm, other ears to hear the parting of grass as teeth come closer. O had no one. The only eyes, ears and nose that were any use to her were her own. And there was another problem: perspective. Her eyes were just above the ground. In the distance she saw shape, change of shape and movement, but it was her nose and her ears that filled in the detail of the shapes and the motion. Her eyes usually insisted that the world stopped at the next stand of grass, or the hedge that bordered the field. Yet she knew that the world wasn't like that. She had been up, and had looked down, and knew that beyond each field was another field, and beyond all fields there was a shining. So she knew that her eyes and ears lied to her; that there was more than the field and the grass; that things were not as they seemed. This uncertainty was dangerous. Rabbits can't live like that. It takes their minds off foxes and stoats.

She wouldn't have lasted the night if another rabbit – a young female too, but older than O – hadn't nibbled her way towards her at sundown. I'll call this rabbit C.* C lifted her head at the squelch of a cow, and saw two ears, plainly those of a small rabbit. C edged on. This wasn't one of the locals. She knew and feared them all, for she was an outcast and might well be killed. This new rabbit was too small to be a threat.

C hopped up to O, looked her in the eye, and then hopped all round. O didn't move. C smelt like O's mother (whom she had sucked but never seen), but without the milk.

C was more interested in O than O was in C. Everything was new and interesting to O, and C wasn't as interesting as a

* For *Oryctolagus cuniculus*.

beetle or a branch because C's body was quite like O's body and O had got to know her way round that already, and even beetles weren't as interesting as the shining, or the hook-beaks of birds or sun through feathers or the creep of loud lice along the snake-roads when you're looking down at them from a buzzard's feet.

C was lonely. She had fled the toxic politics of the local warren and set up home in an old sandy warren at the foot of a sycamore tree. The tunnels were fusty, and she had dug out her own commodious suite, branching off from the pointlessly grand central chamber. There she had lived for a season, happily alone, forging habits, beating paths, learning flight-distances, calibrating dangers. Then, in the midwinter, she'd been joined by another female, older, one-eyed from a fight, clumps of fur clawed out of her coat – another casualty of a big boy's power-play. This other female took up residence in the big hall, and C was grateful at first for the company. But it wasn't much better than being on her own – though there was an extra set of senses for stoat-detection, and an extra set of legs for stamping and kicking. The old female never wanted to play, cuddle or graze, and shouldered C off the clover. She wasn't family.

So when C saw those ears, she wondered if they might make life better. She pushed O towards the sycamore tree. O wouldn't go. Why should she? There was enough right here. More than enough. And it had been a big day. She didn't need entertainment, but if she did, a ladybird glistened on the groundsel, and chaffinches were arguing about territory and sex. O preferred to lie here, her eyes scanning the grass, the hedge and the edge of the wood, trying to work out how the level bolted on to the vertical: how the dimensions slotted together; how *space* worked.

C loped off, disappointed, turning once in a while to see if O was following.

Big though the day was, there wasn't much light in it, and the earth soon inhaled what there was. As the light went into the ground, it drove things out of the ground – things happier in the mortuary light of the moon, which now draped a thin sycamore-shadow over O. The hedge-bottom rippled: a family of weasels like the last small waves on a beach. A badger bumbled through the wood, scratching and snuffling and sucking up worms like spaghetti. A white thistledown owl wafted over the field, dropping from time to time to grip and carry a vole to a ruined barn. O knew, from far down in her brain – from the legacy of millions of years of ripped and scared ancestors – that the waves and the bumblings and the waftings might mean the end of her. *Her! I!* And in the fierce night she knew that there was a *she*, and that *she* wanted to go on sniffing and hearing and seeing the world.

Many – perhaps most – realizations of self get no further than this: they are birthed by the thing that kills them: the teeth, the talons, the tumour, the virus. But O was lucky. For C had seen the waves and the wafting too, and her loneliness and a wild kindness, which is common and hugely more powerful than selfishness, drew her out of the warren and back to O's stand of grass. This time O, knowing that the self was nothing by itself, followed C into the wood.

There we can leave them for the moment, with O learning the languages of touch, tenderness and self-interest, and the etiquette which keeps the balance between them. She learned to titrate her fear against the size of the danger and the need for food. She learned the borders of C's world – much smaller than the world she knew herself – a world bounded by stout hedges, a dairy farm and a roaring road, and full of dread and the pleasures of clover and sorrel. The dread gave no piquancy to the clover, as approaching death makes wine all the finer for us.

A man had watched O from the moon-shadow. He came from time to time. She knew when he was there. He always stood or lay in the same place. He'd flattened the grass down there, as deer do when they lie, and sometimes, when he wasn't there, she grazed around it, sniffing the staleness which lay thick on the ground.

~

This man was not Ken.

Ken, having nothing else to nurse, was nursing resentment, a plan, and a can of white cider.

On the day of the ferret's death he'd gone back at night to the king's warren, pulled the guts out of the tunnels with a stick, and put the surviving ferret down. Nothing happened. He wasn't surprised. But they'd be back. A palace like this wasn't readily abandoned.

They didn't come back. Not the next night, when Ken was there again with his ferret, nor the next, nor the next. The king had smelt more than the stink of an impure weasel. He'd smelt an un-wild malice. Though Ken had been to the warren many times before, something had changed. This stink would never clear, however many babes were born in those tunnels; however many sunlit evenings the king spent basking outside; however bright the crocuses on the bank.

So the king, with his queen and a few ragged survivors

who'd struggled out of the nets and hidden in the brambles and the bracken, moved a couple of woods away to an old rabbit city, thought undesirable because it was semi-detached – it shared walls with a colony of badgers. Badgers would happily eat a nest of young rabbits, but the rabbit tunnels were deep and too narrow for badgers, and the rabbits that had lived there had taken to having their young far underground rather than in shallow, sock-shaped stops, and by and large the badgers didn't bother them.

Now the old city stood empty, with cobwebs over the tunnel mouths and green bones sticking out of the piles of spoil and conker trees a drip-drip-dripping, and someone had dumped a pushchair full of asbestos tiles in the stream at the foot of the mound. But it stank of mould, not malice, and would do for the moment.

The rabbits scratched up the floors until there was fresh earth, and ran hard up the tunnels like plungers in a syringe to push and pull the old air out, and rolled on the new earth so that their hair stuck to it and made the earth their own, and grazed in the field on the other side of the fence and left their droppings around the entrance to the tunnels, for home's not home until you've defecated in it.

Mentally, rabbits are robust, adaptable animals. They are good at both learning and unlearning. Places are as vital to them as hearts, but precisely because places are so important, rabbits quickly become intensely attached to new places, and thoroughly detached from old ones. Things which will do for the moment quickly become the established furniture. Rabbits write history and their sustaining myths very fast. Within the week – and though there were lingering memories of the golden age back at the old warren – the conker-tree warren was their place.

~

Ken didn't know about this warren, and it was difficult for him to find out. The copse was owned by a dyspeptic old farmer who liked to roam his fields with a rusted shotgun, praying for the chance to pepper a malefactor's backside with lead shot. The farm was destitute, and its gates rotten, but the barbed wire strung round the copse was pristine – the finest the supplier had to offer. No expense spared. Three strands of it, on stout posts from a Norwegian plantation, its barbs painted weekly with slurry, so they said in the Rose and Crown, so that anyone spiking himself would have a sporting chance of tetanus.

The only way in was the way the pushchair had come – over plough, through or over a gate now secured with baler twine in incomprehensible knots, and through fifty yards of ankle-deep mud. You have to admire the energy and stoicism of fly-tippers.

So the king and his court were able to settle in, to make the warren smell of themselves, to learn the wiles of the foxes, the schedule of the farmer, the flight paths of the buzzards, the vulnerabilities of the weasels and the habits of the commuters. The king, his libido sharpened by his brush with death, fathered families on three of his sisters, and in due course the families fed a family of badgers in an old fortress a mile away. By the time the young rabbits were eaten the mothers were well pregnant again, and if rabbits could shrug the mothers would have done so.

The land, long locked and still, its seethingness all under-ground, now pushed up and out. It remembered what it had been, and the stalks swelled and stiffened and colour bled back. The hedges and the tree tops squawked, begged and gaped. Organs shuffled and rearranged themselves inside eggs and bodies. The land licked its lips and tucked into its children and grew strong.

There was no spring in Ken's small house. The sun never glanced on the back yard where the old ferret and the new lay coiled. He fed them on pale yellow chicks from a warehouse near Heathrow, and, when he saw feeding mothers pushing into the hedges, on wild bird nestlings. He put the nestlings live into the hutch and watched.

He had not forgotten the warren. He'd worked the other warrens he knew. Nothing. He'd done the rounds of the game dealers, asking if they'd had a big buck with an obvious notch out of its ear. Nothing. He stopped on the roads to look at dead rabbits' ears. Nothing. So he fumed and his mind knotted, and in his fuming he did terrible things and the knot in his head hurt him, but the king and the queen and their entourage, and O, the old matron (now getting sprightly and chatty) and C watched together the renewing of the world and the sullen retreat of the dark, and small ones came to the king and queen's warren and some survived the badgers and buzzards and foxes and trucks and hardened into proper rabbits with hairy feet and brown appraising eyes, and they ripened with the year and the grass and the trees and got tastes and fears and ambitions of their own.

In the evenings the king lay with his queen in the sun on the bank, full of young grass, serene with the calm and jumpy with the fear which both come from having lots of children, and the calm and the fear mixed up inside them and made them what they were.

On one of those evenings in June, when calm for the moment had the upper hand, the king heard a noise like the scraping of a washboard from the other side of the wood, nearest to the road. It was the old jay, garrulous but not neurotic. This was his alarm call.

~

Ken had been on the point of giving up – of deciding that the king had been taken by a fox, a gun, a stoat or a Ford Transit – when, slumped in front of the TV one night, he remembered the dyspeptic farmer's wood. He jumped up, unfolded a map that was on the table, and bent over it.

Yes! Why hadn't he thought of it before? It was the obvious place for the rabbits to go. It was linked to the wood of the old warren by old deep ditches that would have given them cover as they went. It was further than the other warrens he'd staked out, but getting there was safer, and once they were there it wasn't surprising that they hadn't ended up with the game dealers.

He walked straight to the back yard, put his ferrets in their box, jumped into the car and raced off to the wood. It was twilight by the time he got there. The farmer was in the Rose and Crown, and would be there until well after closing time.

~

The king raised his head when he heard the washboard. It might be the fox from the spinney, out to feed her children. But the jay's accent and rhythm weren't quite right for that. It wasn't the drawl of fox-fear. He thumped out a command. Go. Anywhere, but not underground. The other older rabbits didn't need to hear any more. They scattered. The youngsters followed, feeling the fear but not the reason.

The king stayed on the bank, partly out of pride. He needed to show the others that he was steadfast in the face of threats, and he needed to know what those threats were. But there was something else. The king knew, with a certainty far beyond anything that could be conveyed by nose, ears, eyes or any sense that we think important, that something was approaching that might mean the end of things; the end of basking, of fathering, of sweet grass. The air trembled with the knowledge, and the wood and the king trembled with it.

He ran to the top of the bank. There the air from the field reached him. It hadn't bounced between the trees, and so was uncomplicated and easier to read. In the air was the false-weasel stink, and the air had shared its own memory of the king's children's entrails slung down the holes, and the king remembered the heat of red eyes in the dark and the spade slicing the roof from the world so that the sky crashed in, and this could not be borne, and so he thumped and whined and went below to jostle and kick and the last of the rabbits scuttled into the nettles as Ken was pulling the infected barbed wire out of his trousers and jumping down from the gate into the wood.

Ken saw the fresh droppings and the fur from fighting and scratching, and spent a good twenty minutes with his nets, making sure there was no way out. He pegged nets over the mouth of every hole, and surrounded the whole area with two layers of perimeter fence. He took his shotgun out of its case, and both ferrets out of their box. He put the ferrets into the warren, one at the top of the bank, the other at the bottom. He slipped two cartridges into the gun, snapped it shut, pushed off the safety catch, and leaned against a tree from which he could see all the holes. He'd take them all out: every last one. He didn't want to come across that plough and over the wire again, and he was sure he'd found the king.

It was taking a while. He saw movement at one of the holes, and raised the gun to his shoulder. It was one of the ferrets, looking apologetic. It moved to the hole next door, sniffed, and went down. A minute later it returned. The other ferret, a more experienced animal, which had been part of the raid on the king's previous warren, had been down several holes, come out, and now lay grooming itself in the sun, at the spot still warm from the king's body.

Ken was baffled. He knelt down and peered into all the holes. He rolled the droppings in his fingers. Perhaps the whole colony was grazing in one of the fields on the other side of the wood. Yes, that must be it. But if that's what it was, they were early away, and he knew that they might be out all night. It didn't matter. He'd wait for them.

He unpegged the nets, boxed the ferrets, put them together on the other side of the gate, with the wind blowing their scent over the field in front of the farmhouse, where the rabbits certainly wouldn't be, shouldered his gun and climbed up into an old oak tree.

There, I'm glad to report, he spent a very unpleasant night indeed. The just and kindly oak rearranged its bumps and knobbles to align with the sharpest and least forgiving of all Ken's bones, however he shifted; judgemental clouds wept cold and copious tears over his cruelty and his thin clothes; and the wind changed so that he could just hear – as his ears strained for the rustle of rabbits in the undergrowth – the church clock telling how terribly slowly the hours were passing.

~

The king's court had a wretched night, too, huddled together under a blackberry bush, hearing the rustlings that might mean death, and a screech that did. At dawn (which for rabbits, just as for humans, banishes some sorts of fear), the king pushed his nose cautiously out of the thorns, looked over his shoulder to see that the others were following him, and lolloped away.

He was drawing on an old memory from a time of adolescent despair and delinquency when, spurned by the does, his libido turned to travel-lust and, sometimes alone, sometimes with a similarly frustrated friend, he roamed the copses, fields and ditches. There was, he remembered, a small but adequate warren, buried in an ancient hedge. The rabbits there were a mild lot. Perhaps it might do, at least for a while; and even if there were no spare holes the hedge-bottom was secure and dry enough. That's where he was heading now.

It took them an hour, for they tried to keep to dense cover, and so took a roundabout way, and whenever they had to cross open country they waited anxiously at the edge, looking up at the sky for claws and across the field for teeth, tasting the wind, listening for the too-quietness that might mean a fox. But at last they were there. It looked just as the king had remembered, but it didn't smell or sound that way.

They heard the warren before they saw or smelt it. It hummed like a hive, and flies too heavy for precise flying blundered into the hawthorn twigs as they staggered out, drunk on decay.

The king motioned to his people to stay where they were, and crept forward.

The foot of the hedge was so un-right that at first he was overwhelmed by the mystery and his limbs stopped working. Around the warren were five very dead rabbits. Some were studded black and shiny with flies. Some heaved gently with maggots, and their movements looked like breath. But that was not the worst of it. It was horrible to be alive here, and there were three rabbits alive; lying on their sides as if they were mopping up the sun, but with blood weeping out of their eyes, noses and anuses. They rolled those bloody eyes, and the whites were yellow, and the pellets on the ground were red.

The king did not understand that this was rabbit haemor-rhagic disease. He did not know that the virus was desperately contagious and quickly fatal, but he did understand that this was worse than Ken's malevolence, because malevolence can get bored or change its mind or its target or miss, but this thing in the hedge was not capricious and so there was no appeal to it and no chance of it making a mistake. So he stamped and ran as fast as he could across the open field, for the perils of openness now seemed like fresh water, and claws seemed clean. The others streamed after him, hot with his infectious fear.

~

As they were running, Ken was lowering himself stiffly out of the tree. He took a last ill-tempered and mystified turn round the empty holes in the bank by the nettles, gathered up his gun, his ferrets and his nets, ripped his trousers on the wire as he climbed over the gate, and slunk back to the car to find that his stereo had been stolen by a local predator.

For the first time ever he was late for his work at the chicken factory. It wasn't good to be a chicken that afternoon.

~

O, C and the matron, eating new daisies in the meadow by the sycamore, saw the ears of the king's court above the grass. The court had slowed down now, for the horror was back there, and the king made a stuttering advance, stopping to scan, sniff and query. O's wood looked and smelt promising. He could see three rabbits there already, looking relaxed, but they were small females, two obviously young; one older. If only small females were abroad, that probably meant that there *were* only small females there, and that life there was easy: they didn't look like frontier-pushing pioneers. Nonetheless it was best to be wary. He didn't want to lead his tired, scared people into the promised land, only to find that it was full of kicking, biting, jealous giants.

O saw the king's ears flatten as he nosed closer to the wood, more like a cat than a rabbit. She wondered what game this was, for rabbit-evil had not entered her world. She knew nothing of territory or claims. No tussock hereabouts was marked with strident dobs of male musk. So she moved out into the field towards the king. He stopped, and his ears flattened more. Only challengers came towards him. But this was a strange challenger: tiny, brazen and playful. He didn't like it at all.

He couldn't back down. He'd never recover. Already a young buck had started to throw his weight around and look for falterings. He felt the eyes of his people flicking between him and O. He couldn't leave it any longer. Forgetting about guns and buzzards, he charged. O stood her ground. This was an odd game indeed. That big rabbit was going very fast. He'd misjudged it. If he wasn't careful he'd hit her.

He did. Hard. He tossed her with his head. She came down with a thump which knocked all the wind out of her, and then the king picked her up by the scruff as if she were a baby rabbit and flung her about until her skin came away in his mouth and she fell dazed and bleeding to the ground. Then the king knew that there was no threat and was as embarrassed as a rabbit ever can be (which isn't much), and thought briefly that he should kill O so that the people wouldn't have a walking reminder of his misjudgement. In the end he decided that it was best to ignore the little bleeding problem, and, ears now pricked, he marched triumphantly on (though it wasn't much of a triumph).

C and the matron had watched, alarmed but not baffled. They had an idea what was going on, feared for O's life and, when they saw other ears among the dandelions, knew that nothing was ever going to be the same again. Packs of rabbits don't process purposefully across fields in daylight unless they're on the warpath. Usually they're in search of *Lebensraum,* and have come from a hinterland of angst and violence and don't want to conciliate or share. O's body told them enough. They came out of the wood, showing themselves to the king so he could see the signs of submission in their ears and faces and haunches, and took a cringingly wide route to where O lay. They licked her face. She slowly raised her head. They put their noses under her, and pushed her on to her feet. She staggered off with them.

That day and that night the king and his followers celebrated.

O's warren was ideal. And there we leave them, though it should not be supposed that they lived happily ever after.

It was politically impossible for O, C and the matron to stay.

~

Ten years before, a smiling man had drummed his fingers on the table in a Birmingham boardroom and, with the help of a spreadsheet handed round by acolytes, demonstrated that it would be madness not to build a business park on some agricultural land in the West Country. That it included a mediaeval burial ground was, he assured the board members as they studied the figures and the plans, an irrelevance. As were the orchids, the otters and the oaks. It was tedious that they'd have to widen the road through the village to get the lorries through, but there were ways of smoothing that over. Here it all was on PowerPoint, with pie-charts, in case anyone had any doubts.

'Any questions?' he beamed.

'Yes. When do we start?' beamed back his anointed deputy.

~

It wasn't as easy as they'd thought. The villagers didn't go quietly. The offer of a new roof for the community centre didn't silence some of them. The tame MP, bolstered by promises of donations to party funds, had to bluster about injecting life into the rural economy, many rounds of golf had to be strategically lost, many councillors' wives were told to cook their hearts out for the dinner guests, the local papers had an inconvenient spasm of independence, and the corridors of the town hall were choked with whispering men.

When the deal was done druids, mumbling about ley lines and sacred space, were joined in front of the bulldozers by dreadlocked anarchists, pipe-smoking mediaeval historians, earnest twitchers in Gore-Tex, and a retired bank manager, recovering from a lifetime of respectability, who had done a devastating audit of the costs and benefits of the project. And to cap it all, they were fuelled with tea, buns and cheese-and-pickle sandwiches shuttled out by the Women's Institute, who had established a forward command post in a garden shed whose walls were plastered with rotas in spidery writing.

The daughter of one of the golfing councillors came home from east London and chained herself to a digger. The bank manager's son quit his job in the City, chained himself beside her, and a couple of years later a little eco-warrior called Kosmos was born. A priest in a long black cassock declared that it would be demonic to disturb the bones of the ancient dead, and flicked holy water on to the surveyors to exorcise the spirits that possessed them. The local vicar, who had parliamentary ambitions, kept quiet, and his car tyres were deflated every week for a year. A posse of students camped out on the steps of the company's Birmingham HQ. A rare type of tardigrade was found in a log at the site and used as a logo on the protestors' website. A colony of bats looked useful, but they weren't quite protected enough, and the executive director of the company counter-attacked by buying bat detectors for the local natural history society, which unwisely accepted them. When the police dragged off a photogenic girl on prime-time TV, giving her a good kicking in the back of the van for good measure, the questions provoked gave some hope for a while.

It came to nothing. The company wore them down. The bank manager's analysis was mocked by a management consultant with rimless glasses and a battery of computer simulations. The anarchists drifted away to more strategic protests. The cheese-and-pickle sandwich supply withered in the winter cold. The newspapers turned to a new bypass (flagged up by shrewd councillors, tapping their noses, as a useful diversion from the industrial estate). The company planted some trees in Scotland, pledged that the estate would be practically carbon neutral within a decade, and handed burgers to the Birmingham protestors, saying in front of the cameras that they respected their stand, and that it wasn't the protestors' fault that they didn't know the full picture.

The bones were dug up, documented by the archaeologists, and reinterred in a solemn ceremony presided over by a bishop and attended by the chairman's wife in her best black coat. The tardigrades were given a brand new home, with lavishly illustrated information boards and tarmac walkways, and the trees weren't felled or the hedges grubbed up until the nestlings had fledged.

An old rabbit warren somehow survived on the edge of the new estate road. Wandering after their eviction from the sycamore warren, O, C and the matron found it. It was empty. They settled in gratefully.

Over the next week they began to explore. They grazed on the manicured verges, and though they felt exposed from above because the ground gave them no cover, it meant too that they couldn't be surprised by stoats. They learned to ignore the wail and screech of the road. All those sounds were orders of magnitude louder than anything they'd met before, and so to ignore them meant living with divided minds: the crass, the vulgar and the obvious were noted at one level, and discounted, and all the real living (which was to do with silence and the cadences of scent and the comfort of snuggling and the awakeness that comes with the thought of a weasel, and the dew that falls even on poisoned corporate grass) happened in another world, unconnected with the world of the trucks.

There was no night outside the warren. Sickly sodium lights drizzled a sort of day, and the rabbits found this the hardest thing of all. It was a kind of transportation, for the dark was home. Rabbits like to feed in the night and the in-between times when the night and the day bleed into one another. These are better times than the day. The day is just too obvious for any creature of sensibility: too blaring. To live in the day demands a surrender of nuance, and this surrender was painful.

But there were no guns, dogs or badgers. No rabbits with yellow eyes or the swollen, pus-filled, blinded eyes of myxomatosis. O, C and the matron lived as nuns; truncated, ordered, squeezed, cloistered and safe. The man who had watched from the edge of the wood in the days after O had been dropped from the sky was watching here too. He'd manned a barricade during the protests, twisted his ankle in one of the rabbit holes, wondered what would happen to the rabbit colony there, and decided to take his binoculars and his Tupperware dinner to the wood on the edge of the industrial estate a couple of times a week.

The CEO heard that rabbits had been seen on the grass and despatched a photographer to snap them with the chrome and glass ramparts rearing in the background. O duly appeared on the front of a brochure handed out to shareholders at the next AGM.

There had been no straight lines or right-angles in the lives of C and the matron. Everything had curved or billowed. Even a straight-looking stick was, when you got up to it, just lots of knobbles stuck together. Time was marked out by light, dark and heartbeats. Darkness fell when the rabbits went underground; hearts raced at the scent or memory of a fox, and slowed in the evening sun when the wind blew in a safe direction and when C, O and the matron lay together in the dark, chest against chest, hearts in time with one another.

Now it was different. All the grass stems they could see were straight – shaved before they could bend. All the grass was the same species: anything other than the approved version had been killed by chemical sprays, so there were no unruly islands of barren brome, couch, sedge, bent, sweet vernal, dog's tail, fox tail, timothy, fescue, cocksfoot or yorkshire fog, let alone plantains, poppies, hawkbits, vetches, yellow-rattle, scabious, selfheal, knapweed, thistles, docks, buttercups, mosses, or any of the other insolent ragamuffinery of an English meadow. The rabbits' only night was the night they made for themselves by going underground. To create your own day and night – to be your own separator of light and dark – is an unsettling blasphemy, even for rabbits.

All this hurt C and the matron. Eyes built for roundness and variety were forced to follow lines. It was a kind of conscription.

It was rather different for O. She was cosmopolitan, and that meant being attuned to lines. On her very first daylight eye-opening, high up there above the trees, she had seen that the land was all lines: a mesh. And whenever she had seen the droop of a stem in a field she had known that that wasn't the whole truth about the field. She had known this not at the level of her consciousness, but in her being, where everything is that matters. She was a very modern rabbit, and now – though it never amounted to a swagger – had a poise her older companions lacked. The road-curve warren and the antiseptic lawns were more hers than theirs. She grazed nearer to the fork-lift truck drivers when they picnicked, and ate the bits of lettuce they threw to her. She slept more soundly, her head against the ankle of a fourteenth-century swordsmith. In her dreams the growl of the articulated lorries was never the growl of a wolf.

So O thrived, and C and the matron shrank, and one day the old lady didn't return home in the morning, and O and C searched and sniffed for her, and rubbed her place in the burrow with their paws. The old one had never got going in life; had always been muted and reserved; but now she was gone and her place was cold. A colony of two is not a colony. There were no others to warm the cold space. There wasn't the busyness of a normal rabbit community to dilute the emptiness.

The emptiness was worse for C. She had lived with the matron for longer, and the land wasn't as kind to C as it was to O, and because the land wasn't kind, C wasn't kind to herself, and continued to shrink back into the earth.

Then the rains came. Two weeks of rain. Three. Four. Tired, lustreless rain, at the dreary end of its journey. Rain that drowned beetles and then worms and knocked insects out of the sky, starving a generation of summer migrants who left their young rotting in the nest and flew back to Africa in disgust and despair.

The employees in the industrial estate peered grimly through the plate glass, cursing their own lost summer beach-days, and put out buckets to catch the drips that came through the brand new roof. Damp got into the fuse-box, the wi-fi went down and they were all sent home to be miserable there instead – and couldn't come back for a week, for the low-lying roads were flooded.

The roof and the fuse-box might have been permeable, but the concrete and tarmac weren't. The engineers hadn't thought about that, or if they had they weren't telling anyone.

O and C knew that things weren't right. Their tunnels fidgeted with refugee worms and sanctuary-seeking mice and voles. And one afternoon they were woken from an uneasy sleep by water pouring on to them. They scrambled out. They were only just in time. The entrance tunnel sloped down to a sump, and the water there was up to their chins and rising fast. They shook themselves off, stood confused in the down-pour, and finally loped off.

The watcher, rain streaming down his face, saw them go.

O knew where they were going. C was happy enough to fol-low. O knew from her flight that two miles or so away, next to a cider farm, a round mound, topped by a single oak, rose out of the flatlands.

It was not easy to get there. They could not use the ditches, which were all full of water, and the mound itself was now almost surrounded by water – an ark about to float. It took them a while to find the thin dry ramp, but at last they did, and they climbed aboard. Like all proper arks, this one was crowded. As on all proper arks, appetites and ancestral animos-ities were forgotten. Hares huddled next to foxes and voles next to crows. The spirit of the ark didn't diffuse into the waters. Herons, almost too heavy to fly, had crops full of drowned field mice. An otter swam between submerged gates and sprawled on a bank, chewing on a leveret.

A car pulled up near the mound. Like the rabbits, it had

taken a roundabout route to avoid the floods. The driver wound down the window and studied the mound through binoculars. Satisfied, Ken got out of the car, pulled on rubber boots, hung his shotgun over his arm and opened the gate leading to the mound.

The watcher had been waiting, looking like part of the mud, and he stood, smiling, to greet him, for all the world as if they'd arranged to meet for a drink in the downpour. As he stood, he pulled a notebook out of his pocket, peered at the car's number plate, wrote the number down, mouthing the last letters so that Ken could hear them, put the notebook away, and resumed his broad, welcoming smile.

Ken knew when he was beaten. Thunder-faced, he turned on his heel, jumped into the car and sped away into the gathering dark.

It was an uneasy night. The cold and the wet were dissolving the truce between the species. The carnivores had been scrupulous in not eating their neighbours until they were carrion, but when an icy moon sucked the last of the heat from the land, and threatened to suck it from the bodies of the ark-cargo, it was rumoured that a young, thin and yobbish fox had taken a partridge and that a badger, trying to open a curled hedgehog, had rolled it into the flood. Nerves were frayed: but where could the animals go?

There was one other place, thought O: a place right on the edge of her vision when she was in the buzzard's claws. A high field topping a plateau that overlooked the plain and drained steeply to the river that curled round the ark and was now a mile wide. That field, O dimly knew, must be dry. The metalled road climbed up to the field, and in this time of flood was the only way there.

At daybreak the watcher stood aside to let O and C come past along the ramp. He saw them turn up the road and followed them, far enough behind not to frighten them, and near enough to keep them moving if their resolve began to fail.

O's memory had served her well. The high field was planted with oilseed rape. O and C shouldered their way between the densely packed stems. It was dry and warm, and the food was first-rate. They ate, they dug, they ate more and dug more, and by sundown had the beginnings of a respectable home.

Over the next few days, dry under the canopy despite the relentless rain, O and C continued their excavation, licking the soil off one another's faces at the end of each digging day. They hollowed out a home in the middle of the field, and burnished sides of the main tunnels with their bodies, and it was time to stop building and start living.

They did. When the sky had poured itself empty, the field, which had waited long for the chance, ignited in yellow to burn the eyes and green to break the heart. The rabbits gorged on the sun because they knew the dark would come, and lay on their sides at the edge of the fields with their eyes blissfully shut and the fleas jumping in celebration, and when the hill swallowed the sun the rabbits put their tongues inside the stalks and felt the sugar that was crystallized sun ebbing and flowing in a tiny sweet tide; and for a while things were the way things should be, though the chemicals on the leaves made O's eyes sting and her gums blister and if she'd lived long enough would have turned her own lymphocytes against her.

But far, far more than it was a refuge for rabbits and deer and a larder for bees, the field was an entry in a set of accounts: an electronic ledger, to be exact, located nowhere in particular unless it was in the spaces between molecules beyond the outer edge of the Earth or, if it pleases you, in a supercooled warehouse in Ohio.

This entry – though it's not clear what sort of thing it was – had a voice, and the voice barked orders to a man who obeyed, rose one summer morning, put on a boiler suit, oiled a big machine, and prepared to cut the rape.

He couldn't start the cut early: the sun had to dry the field first. At mid-morning a fleet of Land Rovers arrived at the farm and disgorged six cheerful, tweedy, heavily armed men who guffawed and ate their sandwiches in the sun until the combine was ready to go.

O and C were near the middle of the field. The combine started at the bottom, and the gunmen picketed the field. The farmer was interested in the harvest of the tiny black seeds rattling in the pods; the gunmen in the harvest of the mammals and birds that had taken refuge in the field, and in the barrel of beer that awaited them when the job was done.

The combine, guided by signals sent to the air-conditioned cab from a satellite in the suburbs of the moon, mowed the first strip, spitting the seeds into a trailer hauled alongside. Lady Gaga pumped through the driver's headphones. He sang along. The noise of the gathering arms had no rhythm or tone: none of the swish-de-clunk-de-pressity of earlier machines, let alone the swisssssh-zing-pass-the-cider of the old scythe-men. It was mere noise.

The steel arms gathered a young rabbit and a family of partridges from the first strip, from the next a broken-legged pheasant, and from the next a fox cub. A hare, running before the arms, broke cover across the stubble and turned an elegant cartwheel as it was shot in the face. A pheasant rose stiffly out of the forest of stalks and tottered through the air towards the trees. Its wing was shattered by a lead fusillade. It hit a tree, dislocated the other wing, and fell to the ground. It would be food for the bereaved vixen that night.

As the combine screamed nearer, a wind of the sort that makes mid-Atlantic water stand up house-high crashed over O and C, filling their eyes with dust and fungicide and plastering their ears to their heads, and their heads were full of the toneless crash, and though their eyes were dry and red with the dust they were wide open because there were things happening on the edge of the field, and their noses were no use because of the tides of black diesel smoke that curled in with the wind. The earth shook. Mice scrambled to squeeze under the clods. O and C didn't go into their tunnels because they knew arms would reach in and claw them out, and because the quaking earth would fall on top of them, and because home was about nuzzling and safety and all this had nothing to do with that.

It was too much for C. She looked over her shoulder at O, turned round and mewed in her ear, and tried to push her out of her redoubt and towards the wood. But O had had too many moves in her life, and wasn't moving again. O could see the lines of guns, knew what C was about to do, and grabbed her by the scruff as a mother grabs her young. But C shook free and bolted into the desert left behind by the combine, straight towards the legs of one of the shooters.

This shooter was the watcher, who'd accepted a friend's invitation to the shoot, and the loan of a gun, but had mysteriously missed everything he'd fired at – often by a very long way, it was said later, when the beer barrel was tapped. He was no better now. He raised the shotgun, pointed it roughly at C, put the first load a good ten feet behind her, cursed loudly but convincingly, and narrowly missed the trailer with the second. C was halfway to the wood and safety.

Ken wasn't near enough to see the half-smile on the watcher's face. But he was near enough to feel contempt for the man who'd taken his car number, and whom he'd been very surprised and embarrassed to see at the farm that morning. He was also near enough for something else. He only needed one shot. The pellets hit C squarely in the chest. Dead already, she ran five yards before slumping and twitching.

O saw it all. She bolted straight for C, running under the trailer, took hold of her scruff again, and tried to drag her body towards the wood. Ken flicked off his safety catch: he still had one barrel left, and he couldn't miss. He pulled the trigger. There was a dull click. A misfire. Damn! Cheap bloody cartridges. Or perhaps he'd left them in the damp. He fumbled in his bag for another cartridge, and pushed it in. But what was going on now? That madman: the useless bloody shot; the man with the big nose and the notebook; the man who was always where he wasn't wanted – he was in Ken's line of fire. Did he want to be killed? He'd half a mind to give him a load to teach him some manners. Ken shouted something obscene. The watcher turned and smiled again, and walked towards him. Ken should have run to one side so that he could get a safe angle on that rabbit, but somehow he couldn't.

Now it was too late. The live rabbit had left the corpse and had loped slowly into the wood, looking back all the time.

The gunmen cleaned up. There was quite a lot to do. The last remaining strip was dense with palpitating life: everything almost shoulder to shoulder, as in the ark. Some brazened it out, and their paste went into the trailer along with the black seeds. Others took their chance with the guns. Few got past. The Land Rovers were laden and soon the freezers and game pies of Somerset would be full.

It was good beer, and most of it was gone when the midsummer moon pushed out the midsummer sun, and O, drunk on the silence and the sadness, drawing deep on her buzzard-memory, staggered towards the shining sea.

GANNET

Morus bassanus

If one gannet generation is, let's say, twelve years, then it was twenty-five generations ago that an old Icelander, his body built from the bodies of puffins, guillemots, sheep and cod, looked out into the fog rolling into his black beach, pulled on a pipe made from the ulna of the cousin ninety-five times removed of the gannet we're going to meet, and knew suddenly that he was going to die.

I do not know if the pipe had anything to do with the knowledge, but until he drowned that winter he always said that it did, because his grandmother had prophesied that a white bird would tell everyone in the family how they would meet their end.

The grandmother herself, five gannet generations earlier, had a purse made by folding and stitching the leathery grey web of a cousin (a hundred and four times removed) of our gannet. She always insisted that since gannets incubate their eggs under their feet, there was no safer place for her money. And so it seemed. She never gave a krona to anyone.

She read the Bible by the light of fulmar oil poured from a bottle made from the gullet of a cousin a hundred and seventy times removed from our gannet. She rubbed her husband's rheumaticky back, stiff from the whale-killing, with grease from a gannet that had found its way up to Iceland from the shrieking stacks of St Kilda, whose family tree joined our gannet's only when Odysseus was making his way home through other fickle seas.

Our gannet was hatched in the very centre of a shrill gannet city of bayonet beaks and eyes cold as glaciers. This, along with Wall Street, is one of the few places in the world where you can smell unadulterated natural selection. There is no kindness here. It is ruled not by the stern poetry of the sea that lashes and licks and gnaws at the cliffs, but by formulae and spreadsheets. There are very few examples of such simplicity. Competition, undiluted by cooperation for cooperation's sake, is terribly rare – at least in complex multicellular creatures.

Before he smashed his way out of the egg into the squawking web of algorithms, he had known for a while the grating of the colony, the crescendos as hunters returned with full crops, the lulls when foraging parties set out for the sand-eel fields of the Tay estuary and the Farnes, the boom of the waves and the drone of the wind. Territorial tension seeped through the shell. He knew about knives and edicts before he knew about fish or air. He came out fighting and panting, covered in blood and slime, shivering in the blast of the westerly wind which made them button up their coats and blow on their hands in the bus shelters of the dour little town over the Firth, and his first taste of relationship was when his mother vomited a still-wriggling capelin down his throat.

It didn't always seem that way, but he was a favoured one, for his home nest faced the prevailing wind. It chilled; it made him austere. To maintain their body temperature, his parents had to keep their engines running about three times as fast on the nest as the engines of a typical non-perching bird when the temperature is ten degrees Centigrade. But it also made it easier for his parents to catch the updraught that shoved a fast column of air skywards when the wind cannoned into the basalt cliffs of the island, and it would make his life easier when, in three months' time, he launched himself out over the sea.

Fishy white lime from his parents' vents stuck the nest to the ledge, stopping it toppling to the rocks three hundred feet below.

Like almost all gannets, he was an only child. Until he was a parent himself he would share nothing. While he was naked, and in the first phase of his white downiness, his parents took it in turns to brood him, keeping him from the cutting wind and the pale eyes and the beaks of the neighbours, who would have killed him if he'd floundered over their boundary. He began to learn the raucous code of the colony; the way savagery was sub-limated into ritual; the meaning of the waves of sound that rose from 150,000 corrugated throats, rough from the scratch of fish ribs, and broke over the colony like surf; the clack of big horn beaks in greeting as the bayonets were decommissioned for a while; those pale eyes scanning the frontiers of the nest site; croons that might have been affection but were not.

There was much he did not see or hear. The broken birds hopping at the foot of the cliffs, pecking at the rats that hung on them like burrs. His mother hunting three hundred miles away, for the sand eels were failing and the mackerel had not come, and flopping home in the last of the light. Guillemots struggling to rise from a slick spewing from a tanker, preening themselves, ingesting oil and doubling up, mewing, as oil plugged their guts. Gannets, wings mashed by the blades of an offshore wind farm, swallowed by an orca. The solemn walls of grey water driving in from the north. The oystercatchers harvesting sandhoppers under the corpse of an ageing Faroese gannet who'd never fitted in and, deafened by the ticking of his biological clock, did not hear the warning shrieks before his rival's bayonet went home, splitting his carotid artery. The mumble of the big road on the mainland. The thump of boat engines shuddering up the nesting terraces and the clang of winches hauling fish up to suffocate in the hold with their swim-bladders out of their mouths like speech bubbles voicing silent words of outrage. The otters looping along the shore and the whiskery dog-faced seals chasing bass through the kelp.

His education during those weeks in the nest was mainly social. He was enlisted into the spartan ranks. He drilled, learned the rules and watched the execution of the sentences for non-compliance: saw the pierced eyes and torn throats and the flailings in the mud. He knew nothing of distance – of the scale of the ocean, its moods, how far it had to be humoured, and what it did to anyone who overstepped the mark. He did not know that life and death both came from the sea. He knew about place, but did not know that the sea was not a place at all, but the expression on the face of a god. He acquired preferences – for his mother over his father, for she vomited more gently into his mouth; for mackerel over sand eels; for the swelling muscles of his right wing over those of the left, though both were equally strong; for his left eye and left brain over his right, for he felt that the left was truer and fed him more reliable data.

Preferences and attributes do not constitute a person. He was not a person, nor even a potential person. There was no seed in his white downy or black speckled or, later, lustrous white head that could grow to be a self as we understand it. He had appetites, and would seek to reproduce and avoid death; but to have individual appetites and to fight against individual extinction did not mean there was anything *personal* about him. The material reductionists are wrong: the universe is not a machine, and no natural organism is truly a machine; but of all creatures visible to the naked human eye, gannets are the closest to being machines. They are of course sensate, but their sensations do not join to form anything that looks like a story that our gannet might tell, if it had the words, in the first person singular. Gannets enfold in their supremely graceful bodies some universal consciousness, but that, though wonderful, is not such a big claim, for even electrons do the same. And so it might be thought that this story of a gannet is a synthetic thing, with no proper pathos. But no! For far and away the best medium for story is the first, second or third person *plural*: we, you all, they.

From well before the moment of his conception this gannet took his shape from the pressure of others; took his position by way of triangulation from all the other countless entities in the universe. He was part of the story of the gannet-ulna pipe, the gannet-foot purse, the fulmar-oil bottle, the gannet-grease liniment. Part of what now dictated his preferences and foibles and made him sweep low over the wave-tops and have his peculiar form of being in the world was present in the gannets who had watched the continents collide and the seas clot to form the ice caps; and even more of it was in the loins and tongues of the birds that now circled over the colony and braked in the air to put their big grey feet down in the mud and guano next to him.

What and who was this gannet? He was, as we all are, a relational thing. He was the nexus of relationships in which he ate, dived and died. He was, like everything else, *all* story. Take one actor away and the story is tweaked, and might end up dramatically different. There are no sub-plots or cameo roles; no mere walk-on, walk-off parts.

He was now thirteen weeks old. His weight had increased seventy-five times since he hatched, and he weighed a third as much again as his parents. He felt strength streaming up from the mackerel in his stomach to his breast and wing muscles, as if the mackerel were still alive and swimming in him. For weeks he had stretched those mackerel-powered wings, and tried to flap, but there was little room in the colony for practice. For the last four days he had tried all the more. He faced the sea all the time now, leaning out towards it; pointing to it with a strained neck; gazing hard at it for three-minute periods of what seemed like a fugue state, in which he'd ignore all the martial, gorging mania of the colony before unfreezing, shaking his head as if shaking off droplets of dream, and turning for a while back to the everyday and the immediate. But soon his eyes would fix again on a travelling wave or the furthest horizon, and the neck would reach out, trying to slice into the wave or peer over the edge of the world into whatever was beyond.

Now! Now! Now he flapped without caring what was in his way, though he'd seen what happened to fledging birds who crash-landed in the colony. He felt the creak of ligaments, the slither of tendons, a lightening. He knew suddenly the shape of his wings; that they were aerofoils, not stumps. He discovered vectors. The wind that drove straight into his face from the sea also, if he stuck his wing into it, drove straight up to the sun.

This was too much to take in at once. He twisted back to

look inland. If he had had a soul, you might think it was nostalgia. Then, with an effort, as though facing his fear on a psychiatrist's advice, he turned back to the sea. Then to the land, then to the sea. This queasy indecision went on for half an hour. Then he swallowed many times – which looked for all the world as if he were forcing down his dreads, but was probably just him inflating his air sacs as a car inflates its air bags just before a crash – shook his head violently to get rid of the misgivings, and leaped into the air.

For a moment it seemed that he'd never clear the colony, but just as he was about to graze the heads of the edge-birds a merciful gust took him up, and he was away, gaining confidence and air-knowledge with every wing-stroke, gliding round, higher and further, looking down at everything he had known, knowing another dimension as we may learn other dimensions at death; knowing speed, angles, trigonometry and a new set of rules – physical this time, rather than social; rules that would constrain and liberate.

His parents had fed him until the moment of departure. They would never see him again. They didn't even turn their heads to watch him go.

～

The wind couldn't do all the work for him. The fish-fuel in his wings ran low. Half a mile from the colony, after ten minutes of flying, he flopped into the sea, folded his burning wings and started to paddle due south.

He paddled, alone and fasting, for two weeks. Sometimes he saw other gannets in the distance, but so far off that he barely recognized them as members of his species. Indeed, since his

sense of 'himself' was so rudimentary it is not clear whether
he'd have thought 'They're like me!' if they'd been hunting all
around him. He dipped his head into the water to wash off the
grime of the land, and began to see things below him. Big
mouths sometimes leered close to his legs, and he scuttered
over the water to get away from them. Far below were flickering sheets of silver – too far down for him to know them as fish.
But once a corner of the sheet folded up towards him and he
saw eyes and tails and fins, and remembered his parents'
retching.

On he paddled, far out now in the big-heaving ocean, climb-
ing to the summit of the waves and glissading down into the
valleys. At night he slowed the pace, though the south still
tugged at his chest and was almost a pain. He watched the
blinking lights of the ships that slid through the sea, and when
they were close he felt their throb as an extra heart. Spray from
wave-ridges drenched him, and though the drops rolled over
the grease he diligently applied, his head was frosted with salt.

He couldn't fly. He was too heavy to lift himself off the
water. Though the wind hit the faces of the grey waves as it had
hit the black basalt cliffs, there were no kind updraughts down
here. The fishy fat under his skin and around his viscera
pressed him to the sea. He had to burn it off and get down to
his parents' weight before he could haul himself up and away
in the air.

This was a precarious phase. By the time he was light enough
to rise, he would have used up most of the fuel that had kept
him alive. He had to hunt for himself now, without any lessons.
Towards the end of the two weeks he had tried to dive like a
cormorant after fish he had seen below him, but it didn't work.
He was too buoyant. He needed gravity to help him drill

through the sea-skin down to where the fish swarmed. He had to fly to feed, and he could not fly until he was on the brink of starvation. It was a problem.

It's amazing how few young gannets die at this point. Ours didn't.

One cold dawn he thrashed with his wings and pushed himself forward and up with his feet, and strained his neck up and out in the hope that his body would follow, and instead of ploughing into the wave that growled towards him his body was dragged up; only slightly, but enough to clear the wave-top with his head and neck and breast, and though the wave snatched at his trailing feet it could not catch them and instead he pushed down on the wave. It knew it was beaten and it fell away below him and he spiralled up, leaving the sea behind for a while until he was sure it couldn't reach him.

From up here he could see many fish-sheets – for this was the Dogger Bank, where the fish grazed in a Mesolithic forest, eating plankton that sprang from the dung of mammoths and sabre-toothed tigers – and he drove hard into one of them, not folding himself enough to plunge down among them, but folding himself enough to avoid dislocating his shoulders. A transparent veil fell over his eyes to protect them as he entered the water, and he looked down and knew what he had to do.

It took twenty dives before he killed, and another twenty after that before he killed again. He learned that speed was everything, for his feet could not take him to the great depths of a hunting auk. He learned that his speed in the air on the downward stoop became fish-killing speed in the water. He learned to squeeze air into the bags under his skin: just enough to cushion the impact, but not enough to make him bob back to the surface before hitting the fish.

At first he thought the fish would dive head first into his open beak, as they had done when they spilled out of his parents' gullet, but they didn't. Then he tried to stab them, as he had seen gannets stabbed by gannets back home on the Rock, but the fish-sheets just parted before his beak or, if he touched a fish, the point glanced off harmlessly. And at last he learned his own style: a sideways swipe with a whip of the head, the bill open, like two scythes swinging through a summer field; and when the tingling body of a fish slid over a blade, the blades closed and sheared, and its serrations stopped any slithering.

He learned that fish were best swallowed down there, in the whirling green and blue. They were helped down by the inward rush of the water, made into a torrent by the force of the dive, so that the fish almost did swim into him after all. If he took a fish back to the surface, unpinioned by the weight of water, it became slippery and desperate again, and had to be juggled down the hatch.

The fat had burned slowly, keeping him ticking over, but the fresh fish blood and twitching muscle in his belly were like petrol thrown on his metabolic embers. He flared up and roared south, down sea-roads made smooth by the wing-beats of ages; over the furrowed sea-fields off Yorkshire, where he barely glanced at the Bempton gannets (fishing, he thought, in a stilted, suburban way); off the twittering coast of East Anglia, where the mate of a Baltic bulker ship took a hopeless pot-shot at him from the bridge; well clear of the stain where London spills into the North Sea; turning west at Margate, within sight of chip shops and Regency terraces; along the sedate coast of south England, where, off Swanage, he speared a used nappy and, bemused, carried it to Portland Bill.

At Portland he veered south-west across the Channel, rounding Finisterre and hugging the rim of Biscay, for he was a bird of the light, shallow, frivolous waters of the continental shelves, not at home over the plummeting Atlantic trenches. That meant being suburban himself along the coasts of Spain and Portugal, gagging on the dung and diesel of Santander, grazing on the generous by-catch of the merry little boats of wild Galicia, coasting on a tailwind down Portugal but being bundled up in a squall and nearly slammed into a slave-owner's lacy portico in Lisbon, and being forced by a vicious westerly to paddle for three humiliating days like a pond duck off Cádiz.

~

When the wind relented he saw that he was at a great cross-roads. A steady stream of gannets passed overhead, mostly young, and many in the black juvenile livery. Most continued south; some steered east, encouraged by the prevailing wind through the narrow door of the Mediterranean.

He looked south. He looked east. He went south. Tentatively at first, but soon emphatically.

Anyone watching him would have thought he had made a decision. And in a way he had. But when we talk about decisions we tend to talk as if they are the consequence of reasons, and thus of reasoning. That does not describe accurately why he went south.

He went south. He just did. He went south because he didn't go east. Perhaps he was drawn south by some sort of field – a field that attracted something in him but did not lure the Mediterranean gannets. I suspect so.

Reasons be damned. He nearly broke his neck plunging on to a fish thrashing on the deck of a trawler fishing illegally off the Canaries, and lowered the blinds over his eyes to keep flying through a chafing fog of red Saharan sand. He soared on the thermals that span up when a big lump of bubbling air from Timbuktu hit a steep cold cliff of wind, full of bitter salt and Orinoco greenfly, and flew too high and got breathless and came down to a rock in the swell of a reef to throw up his last three hunts. Out from Dakar he watched a Shetland gannet drown in a net. Out from Banjul he saw ten gannets, mostly from the west coast of Scotland, gorge themselves on a dead shark whose liver had been clinically removed by orcas. Like newly fledged birds, they were too heavy to fly and mooned sleepily around on the water, waiting for the bowel movements that would liberate them. All ten were clubbed by fishermen and fed to dogs.

Off Bissau he was picked up by a tropical storm and hurled across the border into the mountains of Guinea, where he was stunned against a minaret and fell into the courtyard. For a week the caretaker, a gracious and very religious man, fed him on muddy river fish dipped, for reasons that were unclear, in rosewater. On the seventh day the gannet walked away from his bowl, glanced no more at the caretaker than his parents had glanced at him when he fledged, and launched into a sky thick with woodsmoke, mosquitoes and the haze of fried cassava.

A brown river wound through tropical forest shrill with shining birds. The gannet saw fish jumping, and saw their fins and tails cut the surface. But a brown river is no use to a gaze-hunter, and the gannet, tired and hungry (for the well-meant rosewater fish had been few), landed on the water. Water had always been safe. He went to sleep. But not for long.

He felt an itching in both his feet, and lifted them up to examine them. They were like the heads of a Medusa – writhing, not with snakes, but with black rubbery leeches, each six inches long.

The gannet was delighted. Here was food come to him, unasked, and he set about ripping them off and swallowing them. He made quite a stir. That wasn't good.

The gannet had seen that this curious stretch of water, winding gently down to the sea, was waveless. Yet now, as he turned his head to tear the leeches from his feet, there was a wave travelling towards him, small and slow but unmistakable. He was interested. Perhaps it was made by a big fish. At any rate it showed that the river was more alive than he'd feared. Perhaps he could make a living here after all.

And then the wave rushed and towered until it was higher than him and it had teeth – in fact, two lots of teeth – and they grabbed at him and almost got him but he pushed down and away and jabbed the crocodile's eye so that all that the teeth managed to get was one leg. For such a big and messy feeder the crocodile bit it off quite neatly, leaving only a few tendons trailing, and they shrivelled up over the next week, so it wasn't so bad, and the gannet did get to keep the leeches on the remaining foot.

The fish in the shoals of Mauritania and Senegal had been good enough. He could live for a while on the fat they had made, and he meandered down the river, not knowing that rivers run to the sea, but sometimes feeling brine in his eyes when he climbed beside the vultures over the forest that boiled up from the riverbanks. He saw the small islands that were the backs of hippos, the migrating islands that were the backs of elephants, the logs that were crocodiles, and egrets that looked like gannets that hadn't fed for a year. Gunfire from an AK-47 sheared off one of his flight feathers. He watched a purple heron flapping on the end of a line, a fish hook, baited with a live fish, lodged in its gullet. Flying over a town he saw a river, but saw no water because the surface was floating trash. He landed in an inlet, scanning it first for logs with teeth, to find that there were no fish there because algae, growing on the effluent, had starved the water of all oxygen. He dodged stones and sticks thrown by children, ate a dead rat and choked on a tampon. He tried to perch in an ironwood tree, but gannets' legs aren't made for perching, and a one-legged gannet certainly isn't made for perching, so he toppled off, somersaulted down a stairway of branches and had to fight off a honey badger.

That did for trees. Scrambling into the sky, he climbed high above the gibbering canopy, wound along the river until it sprouted many arms to embrace the sea, and flew on and out, past the last trace of the billowing mud, into the blue. And ever after he hunted further out to sea than the average gannet.

That was doubly difficult for him because of his leg. Gannets don't swim down far by paddling, but their feet are useful for the fine tuning of their final rush on a fish once they've made the plunge and are under the water, and so our gannet had a poor success rate with the usual prey. He learned to make up for it by specializing in larger fish. A gannet might swallow ten herring, one after the other, or four large mackerel in a sitting – perhaps nine tonnes of fish in a lifetime. That shows that they've a lot of space in there – and the space can be occupied by fewer but larger fish. Those bigger fish are found further out and further down. Further out meant going beyond the continental shelf. Further down meant going beyond the usual parameters of safe diving. A normal gannet, beginning its plunge at thirty metres, might hit the water at sixty miles an hour. Miscalculation can be fatal, and often is. If the dead gannet you find along the tide-line has a strangely kinked neck, it has probably miscalculated. Our gannet upended forty-five metres above the sea, folded his wings earlier than usual to reduce wind resistance, and often neared seventy miles an hour at the point of entry. His skull, like that of all gannets, was armour-plated, but pain flared inside his head with every dive and he had to steel himself to feed.

These eccentric habits made him a loner. The sea is big, and gannets rely on the eyes of others to find fish. One feeding gannet quickly brings others. But run-of-the-mill fish and run-of-the-mill gannets were of no use to ours. He went ever further out; out to where blue gave way to green and green to black; where the waves were often the height of houses; where big whales with bad breath puffed; where everything had a languid seriousness; where knobbled things with lights on stalks and eyes as big as their bodies sometimes came to the surface out of the dark and the geological ages to die – as if they felt they should see the sun once before drifting down to let the hagfish root inside their chests.

He started to fly like the shearwaters he watched. He became more of a glider than a flapper, learning just how to lift his wing-tips to miss the wave-tops, yet catching the special energy of those tops; learning to untangle the knots of turbulence and release their power.

He followed ships. One of them, with a generous, superstitious and wasteful cook, he trailed all the way to the St Peter and St Paul Archipelago, just north of the equator, where he was coughed on by a booby and sneezed on by a noddy and caught a fungal infection of his air sacs which made them creak when he inflated them and made deep diving painful. He retreated to the eye-burning white beaches of Sierra Leone and the mangroves behind, and he grew portly on crabs and squat warty fish.

Just beyond the reefs where the sea cracked and broke he saw white and black shapes patrolling; up and down, up and down, lazily methodical, sometimes dropping and spearing. A mile away, he felt the messages flick between them, saw birds gather, and understood how the barrage of beaks would tire, slow and split the shoals, turning safe masses into vulnerable individuals. And, more than that, he saw that that was how gannets are meant to be, not hopping like a heron on the silky mangrove mud, cracking shells and wrenching legs and dodging teeth. He wanted his tongue to shiver again with silver, and wanted the comfort of the old engrained gannet languages. He had seen, too, that gannet numbers here were falling; that birds were starting to move north in small groups. He thought (and I think he did think, after a fashion) that this might be his last chance to be a proper gannet, yet he was fearful about joining them. He was a cripple. How would they deal with that? Kindness is not a category for gannets. And was there a territorial issue? Was the air through which they flew their patch and their patch alone? He remembered those birds at the colony who strayed over a foreign frontier.

As he watched, three birds detached themselves from the hunting party, wheeled round and, with a new purposefulness, started to beat north. Our gannet had a mind and a mind's eye, and with that eye he followed them up the strips of coral, along beaches so hot that beached porpoises fried in their own blubber, where crows and pythons prowled the tide-line for fish and iridescent Costa Rican birds exiled and butchered by a storm that started over Cuba. He knew the gannets would pause to feed where a great river spilled mud and flesh and forest insects afloat on leaves; where fish massed around the corpse of a hippo, twice the girth it had in life; where dolphins, blinded by mud, but navigating on sonar, chirruped, and leaped and spun fish into vortices and pushed them so high that they jumped clear of the water and could be snatched by gannets skimming low and pecking the surface as a blackbird pecks a lawn. He knew that behind the beaches the green thinned and the land wrinkled and went grey. Knew that sand, too hot even for flies, stretched on up until it surrendered with bad grace to the Mediterranean. The sea by this grizzled coast was desert too, crossed, like the land, by occasional trains of travellers; fish trudging in desultory lines like camels. It was sea best crossed fast.

When the gannets reached the straits between Africa and Europe they would continue north, he supposed, for they looked like big birds, lusty and bent on sex. Sex meant the north; the cold seas of origin and destiny. Shrieking seas, wheezing whales, winds shrill, sweet and dank, fish welling up in green water, razorbills flying so fast that their wings vanish like the blades of a plane's propeller; mounds of seaweed on the sex rock; grass ripped down to the rock to add to the nest; high summer sun elbowing through the cloud and seeming to follow, as a searchlight, the clouds of herring gusting through grey water; herring-scale mica spangling the granite, which once made a stupid gannet dive into the rocks and die.

It was not our gannet's time for breeding yet, as he knew. There was no itch inside him, let alone the gnawing pain that can be palliated only by reproduction. He watched the other birds, and compared the adults' adroit corkscrewing dives and their fix on a target with his own fumbling, and knew he had much to learn. He knew that he needed tutors, and milestones by which to judge his own prowess. He needed to know when he could make a bid for the cold seas and the seaweed mound.

He dropped his crab. It scuttled back into the mangroves. He flew to the group of feeding gannets.

~

They did not notice his missing leg, and would not have cared if they had. Their relationships were not sexual, incipiently sexual, or emotional. They had no territory and no jealousy. They cared only about feeding, and the more gannets to disrupt the shoals the better. There was no welcome and no resentment. He had not been part of the group: now he was; that was all.

There were seven left in the group, all young birds with no aspirations to breed next season. Two were Icelanders, from Eldey, off the Reykjanes peninsula, where the sky hangs dark as a black velvet cloth about to drop on a coffin. The last two great auks were clubbed there.

One had hatched in the middle of a storm on Mygganaes Holm in the Faroes, and inhaled more sea water than air in her first breath – water blown out of a humpback, flailed to cream by a panicking seal, and hurled on to the nursery ledge by a wave birthed by the collapse of a Greenland iceberg. One was from Sula Sgeir, forty miles north of the Isle of Lewis, the gneiss peak of a submerged mountain and site of some of the most recent gannet harvests, where men, lowered on ropes, snatched youngsters from the cliffs and broke their necks for their grease, flesh and skins. Another had hatched on one of the granite organ pipes of Ailsa Craig, the great gannet fortress in the Ayrshire sea – a sea that is always cold and humourless and often kills sandcastle-building children because it can. One was from the low cliffs of Grassholm, snow white in summer from its eighty thousand gannets, set in a murderous confluence of currents off the Pembrokeshire coast. And one – a capelin specialist with a dangerous taste for squid – was from the relatively balmy Breton colony of Rouzic.

Some had been on the wing for two years, some for three. With each day and each dive they became better sailors, naturalists, meteorologists and killers.

Now he was in company, our gannet started to notice his missing leg. The group, of course, wouldn't indulge his preference for big fish in deep water, and he had to learn again how to kill small things. His speed into the water helped him, for the shock wave created by his down-powering head dazed little fish, and he could pick them up without needing to be a smartly twisting swimmer. What troubled him more, particularly as winter approached and the Atlantic started to squeal, was the flying, for gannets use their feet as a second tail, and change the shape and angle of the real tail by pressing on it with their feet.

The others drifted north, but without the resolve of the would-be breeders. He went along, seeing how they trimmed their sails in the mounting winds. He found it harder to knock out the little fish in the choppy water, for the bigger waves mopped up a lot of his energy.

Sitting on the sea off Mauritania one dark night, he heard

the grumble of boulders bowling along a submarine alley. Sometimes a storm starts deep in the valleys of the ocean and belches into the sky. He felt the belch coming; felt it thrum up through his one leg into his bowels; heard this little domestic part of the sea protest at being disturbed at such an hour; noticed a rising so gentle it had to be huge; saw that he now looked down on the lights along the coast road that he'd looked up to at the start of the night; knew he was travelling as fast as flight. A roar caught up with the speeding wave. He was on the summit ridge, but only just. He tried to push off but was caught in a messy knot of air which pinned him to the water. He toppled over the ridge. The wave parcelled him up inside itself and tried to make him like one of the boulders on the seabed, but mistimed its effort and instead hurled him half a mile on to the sand, and then tried to draw him back for a second go, but it was too tired by then and left him among broken things.

Strangely he was not broken. He lay until daybreak in a heap of limbs and fronds, not pulling himself higher up the beach because that's where the jackals were. He rose with the sun. He re-waterproofed himself, pulled his big feathers through his beak to reattach the Velcro hooks that held them together, looked out to the sea, which was scrambling over itself to climb higher and challenge the streaming clouds, and then clambered into the sky himself, knowing that there was nothing for him here.

There was no sign of the others. The storm had split them as they split shoals of capelin. One of the Icelanders was tumbled like pants in a washing machine and was unconscious from the G-force of the centrifuge by the time she hit the only palm tree for fifty miles. There she lodged, and can be seen there still.

The ants have done a thorough job. Her bones are as white as her plumage would have been had she survived another couple of years. A pair of trumpeter finches have raised several clutches in her pelvis.

Gannets ride big winds happily – anything up to force eight. But this was more than force eight, and for our gannet the journey north was unhappy. He struggled to keep the strand in sight. The sea sought always to force him into the Sahara, where the freshest fish were 66 million years old, and though the sea wanted to end him he knew that he had to keep faith with it.

Mexican grit scoured his eyes at sixty miles an hour and dumped peyote seeds in the sand. A hundred years after our gannet's death, peyote would unbolt a Mauritanian tailor's doors of perception and trigger a series of books and, eventually, a thoroughly good revolution. Our gannet's feathers unzipped again. He staggered rather than flew. He staggered through the night too, which is unusual for gannets, going low over the fishing villages in search of shelter, and starting a new generation of ghost stories.

The Canary Isles took some of the storm's blows for him, and as he crossed into Moroccan waters it turned in on itself, wrecked some farms and some boats, and fizzled back into the Caribbean to fulminate and regroup until the next time.

The storm had rammed home to the gannet the shortcomings of footlessness. He now wanted an easy life. He idled for a while off Tangier, noting gannet parties going north to the great – but windy – sardine fields of Portugal. Though life was harder by himself, he was not going there.

He saw that twice a day there was a dead calm at Tangier, when the water seemed stretched and tight, and that twice a day there was a sluice of hot salt water into the cup at the cusp of the continents, and twice a day there was a rush of cold, less salty water the other way, into whatever lay on the other side of the straits.

It seemed gentler on the other side. Whatever the sea was doing the wind fussed and thrashed and tried to hustle him east through the gap. This time, he decided, it was best to do what the wind wanted, and one brisk January day he let it take him.

~

On average the Mediterranean is easier than the Atlantic, but as all sailors know, the Mediterranean is capricious, and in a moment can change its mood from it's-sunny-and-I-hope-you're-enjoying-your-ice-cream-have-one-on-me, to homicidal. And, as Odysseus knew, there is more agency in this sea than in others, and the agency is often focused, malevolent and personal.

For two seasons the agent's eye, which no doubt followed the gannet, was kindly. The gannet learned how to slide down the high oregano-scented draughts which whoosh from the little white Moorish villages clinging to the sides of the Sierra Nevada on to blocks of sardines half a mile wide and twenty feet deep. He taunted the humourless fishermen of Marseille, for whom anything is too much trouble, flirted with the tuna-men of Sicily, who crossed themselves when they saw him and threw him fish guts clogged with long white worms, and was almost worshipped by a Greek priest who had spent his life in a Byzantine chapel grappling with Poseidon on behalf of the Virgin of the Brine. The gannet hunted the rippling silver olive groves of the Mani for half a day thinking they were the sea.

He was lonely. He longed for other wings in the strange gull-lessness of the eastern Mediterranean, where even the few gulls are silent; where the only sound is the hiss of the wind in the olives, the lisp of the tide and the clunk of sheep bells. In his desolation he took to buzzing the scavenging crows and winding up high with the eagles.

In the Mediterranean, the sea (that Greek priest was fond of saying) is listening so hard to something (presumably something very old and important) that for months at a time it forgets to breathe. Then the fish gasp, the crabs sweat and the jellyfish stew, and it can be trying unless you know what to listen for, too.

The gannet didn't know, so on his first turn around the Mediterranean he hurried past the dissolving pillars that propped up for a day the hubristic delusions of empire, past the great cisterns of modern wretchedness that will soon crack and flood us all, past all the might-have-beens, past ships bristling with guns as the black sea urchins on the harbour walls bristle with spines – where the sea wasn't listening, but was just too ashamed to breathe, for it should often have intervened and didn't – and out the other side, to Egypt, where for miles the sea smells of the smoky mountain rain of Ethiopia, the burned red pots of Middle Egypt, the Christmas pudding spices wrapped round the viscera of pharaohs, and the potent urinals of Alexandria.

It was here, one green-blue-white spring day, with the bullrushes girding up their loins in the Delta and the little reef fish coming out from wherever it is that little fish go in the winter, that the gannet saw, far off but unmistakable, another gannet: a small but confident, self-possessed, tidy, two-legged gannet.

The apparent self-possession was skin deep. This bird, a female from St Kilda, was, like our gannet, a refugee from the Atlantic, come here in the hope of quieter fishing and a less turbulent adolescence. She was marking time until she was ripe for breeding. When she navigated coolly towards our gannet she was playing no game; not playing hard to get. She had no interest in his gametes, but she did have an interest in his knowledge of fish movements and his ability to spot and split shoals – and, it must be admitted, a minor interest in his company.

She landed on the water beside him. They clashed beaks. The alliance was sealed.

It was not a romantic alliance. It was not even, in the contemplation of either of them, potentially romantic. Even if they could contemplate, foresight of that sort was beyond them – though they certainly foresaw some things. They must have had in their heads a map of the northern seas from which they had come and to which they would return. Combine an intention to return with the knowledge that the route back will be more or less the route out, and you have something that looks suspiciously like a plan.

The alliance was a sort of friendship – a sort that we sometimes have. No doubt it was tinged, as are many of our friendships, with the moral blight of reciprocal altruism. But not all our friendships and loves are disguised selfishness, and this friendship wasn't either. As gannets sometimes soar, surf, play and cluck for mere, sheer joy, even when it uses up hard-won calories and gives no conceivable selective advantage, so this friendship had elements that were not mere by-products of an evolutionarily intelligent strategy, or bait to encourage the gannets to behave in ways that would improve their reproductive fitness. It was often quite the other way, in fact. The friendship sometimes nudged them towards stupid, dangerous, genuine altruism.

Often they were wingtip to wingtip. They never shared food: they always bolted their own catches. But that was in this sea of ease and plenty. A harder territory might have made them generous, as it does for some humans. On the water at night, as big shapes swung under them, the stars were reflected so clearly on the sea that whether they looked up, down or around, the birds saw only stars and it was as if they were at the very centre of the dome of the heavens, and so they sometimes got the sort of vertigo that in humans would be called existential angst or poetical sensibility, and one would paddle up to the other for a beak clash and a reassuring head-shake.

Though they did several full circuits of the Mediterranean, and paused in the Peloponnese every Easter, for two years they were mainly North African birds, beating up and down the blazing glacier-white beaches of eastern Libya, just across the water from Crete, and steering well clear of Tripoli, whose sewage goes untreated into the sea. Here, not far from Egypt, there is no respectful negotiation between land and sea, but the sort of tense standoff that is bound to end badly, and in the winter often does. Here, when the spring migrants start to stream over, or in the hammer-and-anvil heat of the summer, it sometimes seems as if the desert slips meekly under the sea. But it is not so.

There is a struggle for sovereignty, and though the outcome is inevitable, the land puts on a brave show. It corrals sea water in bowls of rock and turns it into salt, which it then blows back into the sand sea that ripples for two thousand miles. It land lashes the sea with sharp-edged silica and blows dust into its eyes.

All this is insult, not injury. It affects neither the sea's aim nor its strength, but redoubles its resolve.

That resolve is shown most often in the winter. The fury is so great that many sea people are crushed by the sea itself as it avenges the slights of the summer and asserts its rule.

It was February. It had been a good day's hunting, and the gannets were resting on the water somewhere east of Algiers, so heavy with fish that if they tried to rise from the surface their toes trailed in the sea.

It was a bad time to be full.

There was no squall; no petulant flare-up; no dark vengeful cloud combing the ocean for a victim or a great wave turning to pâté everything in its path. Just a sudden tightening of the sea's skin until it was taut as a drum. The gannets' three feet would have gone rat-tat-tat if they'd landed on it.

The female was at the centre of the drum. The sea clutched at her legs and pulled them apart until she was nearly split. Then the sea itself split, right where she was. There was a rip in the drum-skin, and down she went into it, and it closed over her head. She never had time to scream. Our gannet, fifty yards away, felt the sea relax, for its job was done.

A human observer would have been more appalled by the lack of ceremony than by the death itself. There is something obscene about a quick, quiet, unannounced, unmarked death. It is an offence against life in a way that a wailing, swearing, struggling descent into the dark is not.

Our gannet was not appalled. He did not think the death was unfair or improper. He was lonely, disorientated and baffled, but alive and full, and those were the main things. He did one more circuit of the Mediterranean and then, entirely without self-examination or comment, enacted his plan, beating along the coast of southern Spain and out into the Atlantic, and swinging north.

~

Just offshore from a Portuguese cork wood he met a group of similarly north-bound gannets, most of them in the clinical white dress that declared them physiologically adult.

Like our bird, most of them were realistic. They were second- or third-year birds, and they knew they would have to serve an apprenticeship before being admitted to the prestigious Reproductive Club. They did not resent this requirement. They knew that membership entailed very onerous responsibilities, and knowledge of an esoteric corpus of law and custom. The knowledge was rigorously tested; the responsibilities viciously policed.

There was, naturally, a tug back to the rock where each had been hatched, but it was easily overridden by the tug of companionship. So our bird, who had always reckoned on going back the way he had come and bidding for a pitch on the Bass Rock, was beguiled up the west coast by the Hebridean birds and threw his lot in with them and with a flat-topped pillar, pounded by surf, inaccessible by boat, whirring with puffins, and patrolled by seals, basking sharks and killer whales.

The group got there in April: a shining spring, mild on the land and sizzlingly cold in the sea.

The sun got to work. Fish which had been slow and deep throughout the winter slid to the surface and quickened. The birds waiting for them knew that the more they could kill now, the better their own chances of successful reproduction, and it was erotic energy in their wings.

Our gannet was not tyrannized by his loins, but he was here to practise, and he practised diligently. He killed manically and ate ostentatiously, perhaps hoping that a female would notice and remember. Though not a member of the Reproductive Club, he was a member of the Parents-in-Waiting Club – an equally well-defined group, which has an exact counterpart in every human society. The members studied the colony, learning how the breeders behaved, and wondering if there might be space just *there* next year, if they reached the pillar early. They made no serious bid for any territory, but pretended they had, trying out the threats and skirmishes that one day they would use in earnest. They displayed as teenage humans constantly do, and engaged in incomplete copulations.

That was our bird's spring, summer and early autumn: playing at being grown up, learning the rules, refining the temperament necessary to service a mortgage and do the school run; enjoying the sight of gannet bodies caught in abandoned fishing tackle because that might mean a lusty widow and a few square feet of cliff.

It was a blithe summer after the traumas of Africa and the Mediterranean. The mackerel came early, stayed late, and were shallow. The local seals were helpful in pushing them up within striking range. Our gannet never noticed that he was one-legged now, and no other birds seemed to do so either. His play-sex was no more ridiculous than anyone else's, and he made up for his clumsy swimming by swashbuckling beak-craft – a skill that would stand him in very good stead the following season.

It was a summer without humans – or without the near sight of them. An occasional distant ship, a sky criss-crossed by vapour trails: that was it. They got us in their diet, of course: our herbicides, pesticides, coolants, deodorants, fuels, batteries, insulators, tyres, antifreezes, scents, plastics and wonky commercial genes. We were in every mouthful and every cell. We coursed through every capillary. We poisoned, disrupted and blighted. There was hardly a gene whose expression we didn't affect. We flicked genes on and off as a naughty child fiddles with a light switch, and we weren't even trying.

The Parents-in-Waiting Club, having surveyed the territory, identified the local feeding grounds and learned the social mores, went south in July, to Biscay and beyond, to the places they had roamed when on their gap years. And later, when the mackerel went, most of the colony went south, too. They weren't following the mackerel. The mackerel would dive deep in the cold. But there were other things to kill.

Our bird glanced at Gibraltar, remembering for a moment, and pushed on south where, rolling with the punches of the winter wind somewhere off southern Morocco, he bided his time. He did not in any way consider his options, for it seemed to him that he had none. He had to get through the winter in fighting condition, head back up to the colony, establish a territory and find a mate. That would be a good season's work. He did not expect to raise a chick that year. Parenthood was a big thing. Its foundations had to be laid carefully.

As he worked his way up the west coast of Scotland on a bitter day in late March, the wind thick with lather, he passed Ailsa Craig. It was already speckled white. Many gannets had been there since January, huddled on the ledges, heads tucked under wings out of the razor-winds which tried to shave the birds into the sea.

Our bird gave the Craig barely a glance. He had already invested a good deal of time and energy in the Hebridean rock, and the investment was not transferable.

To the binoculars and pie-charts of even the most expert zoologists the behaviour of the Ailsa gannets and the Hebridean gannets was identical. But at gannet-eye level the cultures were dramatically different. Gannets from the two colonies were genetically compatible, of course – though in a few million years, given some more cultural isolation, even that compatibility might wane. Had our bird fallen in with Ailsa juveniles when he was a young, impressionable, malleable bird he would have joined the Ailsa club and become an Ailsa bird, too. Now it was too late. It wasn't just the particular ways of bowing, curtseying, threatening and retreating that divided the two colonies. Nor was it the knowledge of the necessary natural history – the movements of the shoals and the shifting of the tides: that could be picked up fast enough. It was, more significantly, what in a human community would be called loyalty: a visceral tie to tribe and place whatever their demerits. It was this, rather than the cost of real estate or the supply of sand eels, that kept the Ailsa birds shivering on their patches instead of basking among the peonies in Alderney.

A day after passing the Craig, our bird arrived at *his* rock. As yet it was not fully his. He had committed himself to it; it had not committed itself to him.

The patch he had had in mind – a bare sloping face on the northern edge of the colony which might yet be made secure for an egg and a nestling with a good bit of engineering – was already occupied by a confident-looking male who had started the necessary works. It would not be easy to displace him, but a plan that had gestated for the best part of a year could not be summarily aborted. Our bird approached, but with fatal tentativeness.

Among gannets, as among humans, swagger counts for more than worth. It took one belligerent bow to see our contender off the site and back into the air.

He remained in the air and perched sullenly on the margins for two uncomfortable and humiliating weeks. His testosterone didn't know what to do. Should it ebb in the face of his failure, or flow to maximize his chances in the time left? He was about to give up when an illegal trawler intervened, enmeshing and drowning ten feeding birds. Most were females, but there were a couple of males, and our bird noted a lone young female at a rudimentary nest looking expectantly out to sea, shuffling with the embarrassment of the bereaved. He alighted next to her. She took no notice. He shook his head and stretched out his neck. She turned away to the sea. He tried again and again, and at last she turned and took a depressed step towards him. He reached out his bill and touched hers. She did not object, but turned away again. Emboldened, he bit the nape of her neck. Again she acquiesced.

Now was a crucial time. She had made no pledge, and other would-be suitors were gathering. Unless he pressed his advantage, all was lost. It meant leaving her – and her site – to the attentions of those others, but he had no choice. He launched and made off with all speed to a nearby patch of sea where, that morning, he had seen a mess of floating seaweed.

There it was! The cornerstone of a new life, bobbing among the plastic bottles. He snatched a beakful and was off back to the rock.

He was only just in time. The female was being courted aggressively – rather too aggressively for their own good, since she was in a sensitive condition – by two of his fellows from the Parents-in-Waiting Club.

Though there was no betrothal, our bird had gone further along the rocky road to copulation, and since the others had no very obvious advantage over him, she decided that the first to come should be the first to serve. She accepted the seaweed, he bit her neck, they fenced with their beaks, and the deal was done.

In the eyes of the male it was, first and foremost, a deal for the land, and only secondarily a deal for the female herself. She sensed his unreadiness for fatherhood, and he knew his unreadiness himself, and though we might have thought that since she had expected to have a chick that season she might have pushed our bird into family life, it was not so. Her previous partner's sperm was pooled inside her, and though she ovulated efficiently, the sperm, exhausted by a dose of hydrocarbons from contaminated mackerel, could not stab through the egg membrane. It was just as well. Another bird's child would have complicated the relationship and worn our bird down.

With no chick to feed, he could concentrate on defending the territory. It was not so hard. Once the title deeds have been properly drawn up, there is seldom any systematic attempt by outsiders to dispossess the legal owner, and though he watched one such attempt end in a two-hour tussle, a lost eye, a number of stab wounds in the head and neck, and a plummet on to the barnacles three hundred feet below (the two birds still wrestling when they broke their backs), he had no bother himself. He reined in his libido; he worked on his relationship, which became stronger with every beak clash; he got to know the neighbours; he looked patronisingly on the unpaired club members; he thought of next summer. And, most of all, he built the nest, and became more tethered to that patch with every bit of bladderwrack and mummified puffin chick, every strand of shredded carrier bag and colostomy bag and Coke can and other badge of human shame that he grafted into the structure. This would be his nest far more than his mate's. He spent more time building it and defending it. It defined him far more than it defined her. Her place was her oviduct. His was the nest. If you could have asked him what he was and where he was he would have nodded his beak at the nest.

For a summer they played house, played parenthood, acted out responsibilities that they did not have until the grooves along which their lives would eventually run were engrained in their habits, their prejudices and their psyches. When they caught fish they were doing it for an imaginary chick. When they beak-fenced with one another they were ensuring that next season – they'd always lived their lives for *next* season – their relationship would weather, for the sake of that chick, whatever storms the Atlantic flung their way.

It was a kind summer. The mackerel came early and again stayed long. The birds did well. Fat padded out their necks and cuddled their kidneys.

Then it was September, and again the mackerel started to fade, and our bird tweaked the nest again and defecated one last time, and copiously, to cement it to the rock against the gathering winds, and knocked his bill against his mate's to say that she was his and he was hers and that next year it would all be for real. He took off, looked down on his handiwork as a DIY fanatic stands back to admire his shelves, and went to the waters of the Western Sahara.

We need not follow him there. His story had straightened

out, and nothing happened there to make it swerve. He was marking time now, but he bore his story due north in February (early, just in case anyone else was thinking of putting in a bid for *his* place).

~

He spent a cold and anxious February on the rock, scanning the sky for the female. In her absence and in his anxiety he began to transfer to her some of his devotion to the nest, and whenever he added a ferry ticket or a surgical mask to the structure he thought of it as a beak clash.

Did she think of him as she fished and soared, weaving between the Canary Islands? If she thought at all, surely she did. Not as a lover, no doubt, but as a part of her self, like a foot, or part of her story, like the forthcoming journey to the Hebridean rock where her life would be consummated.

In March she arrived. She called out of a ball of mist as she approached, and he knew her voice and called back to the mist.

They spent three days and nights reconciling, tracing the winter journeys of one another recorded in the smell of their preening oils, and seeking constant and exhausting reassurance that the winter had not prised them apart; that the plan was still in place; that the story was still afoot.

They were eventually reassured, and in due time, after the seemly courtesies and a day of sex, a single egg was delivered. The violence all around them – the jabbing, the threatening, the constant standoffs, the Jurassic coldness – were potent sexual fuel, for the violence was, most of the time, sublimated, and it made the birds' reproductive hormones boil over. A gentle, sedate gannetry would be a sterile gannetry.

Gannets do not sit on their eggs. They have no brood patch for the job of incubation. Instead, they stand on them, enveloping them with the leathery web between their toes. It's a risky business at the best of times, and first-time parents in particular often get it wrong and break the egg. That's what happened here.

It was tiresome, but not a catastrophe. It was early in the season, and there was plenty of time to try again. Another egg duly emerged. The same happened. It happened a third time, and a fourth – by which time high summer was becoming low summer, the gannetry was full of fluffy reptilian chicks, and the mackerel were getting scarce. The birds had missed the boat.

It is tempting to rush to judgement. Various pollutants, including organochlorines (with which the apparently pristine seas around the rock were awash) have been implicated in pathologically thin eggshells in gannets. Perhaps it was that. Or perhaps the female had a defective shell gland. Or perhaps our bird had a chromosomal defect or a mistranscription of a base-pair sequence that meant that all eggs to which he'd contributed were doomed. If so, perhaps perfluoroalkyl substances in the sand eels his parents or grandparents had eaten were the cause. We can't know.

What I can say is that both birds left the rock early that season, flying south together, and that the male did not fly round and look down at the nest this time, and that neither of them looked back, and that they flew slowly, as if their wings were heavy, and that when a former club member returned to the rock next March he found the nest empty, and raised in it a single raucous truculent chick. And that I do not know if this story is a tragedy.

OTTER

Lutra lutra

Twilight over meadow and water, and the evening star might well have been shining above the hill but would have been invisible because of the neon light flooding the sky from the new conurbation.

There had been a heron on this stretch of West Country river. An imaginative child had called him 'Old Nog', but Old Nog had died last season from liver adenomas – a result, said the conservationists, of a long and increasingly blighted life eating fish whose bodies were full of polychlorinated biphenyls and organochlorines.

The family of white owls who used to hunt the meadows, scanning them grid-square by grid-square, had fallen foul of the toxins, too. Their mice, voles and shrews accumulated pesticides and herbicides, and slowly the owls' hormones were shut down. There had been seven eggless seasons, and then the adults, within a few months of one another, started to lose the sensation in their feet. The numbness crept up into their chests, and their toes lost their grip, and an owl who can't grip is dead, and so they were both dead now, one of them dried and mummified inside a tree, and one of them eaten by a carrion crow who gibbered and died himself.

There had been a bridge over the river here since the Middle Ages, but the mediaeval stone bridge was too narrow for the lorries that carried ready meals and mobile phones into the deep countryside, and so it had been replaced by an award-winning concrete arch with no holes for owls or bees.

Had the owls still been here they would have found it hard to hunt in the roadside fields, for day and night the road's clatter drowned out the rustlings of the small mammals through the grass.

Just downriver from the bridge there had been thirteen great trees – eleven oaks and two ashes. The ashes had gone the way of all ashes, and all but one of the oaks had been felled by a zealous farm manager, hoping to make way for a chicken farm. In the end there was no money for the new project: there had been some miscalculation, and the holding company was seeking legal advice.

The remaining tree straddled the river and the remnants of the wood. On the river side its roots formed an arch, most of it underwater. This arch was the main entrance of an otters' holt.

The bitch otter lay curled there now, three grey cubs the size of moles hanging on her nipples, each shoving the others as it tried for a better position. Their father was a long way off. A couple of nights ago he had breached the defences of a trout farm, was full for the first time in months, and was having an unusual daytime sleep inside a drainpipe.

The river had long been tidal, washed twice a day by salt water sluicing up from the wide estuary where two rivers met, porpoises jumped, and clouds of piping birds twisted under the direction of one big mind which could not have fitted into the tiny skulls of any of them. Sea fish had been carried up with the tides into the pool by the oak tree; mullet sometimes, and even tiny flatfish. They could not have lived there long, and they never got the chance. Drowsy and moribund in the fresh water, they were easy prey for the otter dynasties. Salmon had climbed the river too, pausing often, and often fatally, in the pool on their way to the gravel spawning grounds.

There were no tides in the river now, for there were barrages in several places downstream of the holt – blockages as fatal to the functioning of the river as a tumour in a length of bowel. Not only did sea water not come up, fresh water found it hard to reach the sea. The river clotted and stank in summer. Algae bloomed and suffocated the fish. The kingfishers left. No salmon had been seen in the pool for forty years.

Why did the otters stay? That's easy. They stayed because it was their home. But times were lean, and otters are physiologically frenetic. When the bitch swam in cold water, her basal metabolic rate was four and a half times that of a domestic dog mooching round the kitchen. That burned a lot of fuel. And fuel was scarce. Freshwater invertebrates had been decimated by the chemical weapons of industrial agriculture, and with them had gone many of the larger organisms higher up the food chain. Forces outside the river had taken out most of the rest. Eels, for instance. The bitch would have lived mostly on eels if she could. Her West Country ancestors had done. But now it was rare to catch an eel of any size in the river. The last one had tasted of brake fluid and she'd left it to rot. Where else could she look and teach her cubs to look in their year of closely supervised apprenticeship? There was the land, of course. There were rabbits, frogs, the odd wounded pheasant, and farms where the hens weren't always locked away; but getting to them was hard and dangerous. The bitch had left two toes in a trap outside a hen-house, and still didn't swim straight because a farm dog had got a mouthful of tail. She had to travel harder, play and sleep less, dodge more shotgun pellets and know far more habitats than her forebears in the halcyon days. Her cubs would be manic from the moment they were weaned. The farmers' balance sheets had transformed the ecology and psychology of this otter family.

The bitch wrestled free of her cubs. They were still hungry, and mewed in complaint. But she was hungry too, and knew that if she did not feed herself, her milk would dry up and the cubs would die. She slid out into the pool, scouted vainly for anything edible, and swam upriver to some shallower pools where there were sometimes small trout. Nothing. Perhaps one of the few surviving eels in the ditch? No: the ditch was dry. Frogs among the reeds where the bullocks went down to water? One, barely big enough for her tongue to notice. She found a slug. It revolted her and she spat it out with a hiss at the world that had forced her to this. It was said that a hundred years before, a relative of hers had in this very place, in just half an hour, caught and eaten six small trout and two eels. The bitch hadn't had that much in a week – and this was the lush season, when the land and water should have been stuffed with calories.

She followed the track of a rabbit through the grass (one species of grass here: a century earlier there had been nine, and another eleven plant species among them), hoping for a nest of youngsters. She found the nest, but a vixen had got there before her, and there were only clumps of fur and beads of blood. Back to the river, to a stinking tributary fed by a waste-pipe. She rarely came here. A dead roach floated at the edge. Now mad with hunger, she swam across and grabbed it. It writhed. It was alive with maggots. She spat that out too and rinsed her mouth.

She knew she could not leave the cubs for long, and set off back to the holt. On the way a mallard duckling fell too far behind its mother, and all its mother's flailing and pecking could not save it. It was enough for one nipple. Two of the three cubs died that night, going first cold and then still. The mother could not bear to eat them, though it would have made sense.

She kept them by her side for five days, pressing against

them, willing them to suck, and only when the smell was unbearable did she take them tenderly in her mouth and drop them in the river for the rats and the crayfish.

The dog otter never met the surviving cub. He died, as fate would have it, on the same night as his two offspring, for he made the mistake of returning to the trout farm after his gluttony and his sleep. He picked his way cleverly around the gin trap and rejected the fish laced with warfarin, but when a spotlight blared into his eyes he stood blinded and transfixed for just long enough to fall to the twelve-bore shotgun fired from a bedroom window. It was a criminal offence to shoot him, and he was buried discreetly in the wood before the sun rose.

~

Even without the competition of two siblings, it was a struggle for the survivor, and it was a scrawny apology for an otter cub who, one moonlit, neon-lit, lorry-laden night in July sniffed tremblingly out under the oak arches for his first swimming lesson. He was ill-equipped for an otter's life at the best of times, and this was far from the best of times. How can you teach an otter to fish when there are no fish? How can you get a cub to swim and lope miles a day on an empty stomach?

It was an inauspicious start, and on his second outing it got worse. Crossing the bridge as he emerged was a party of snowy-haired ramblers from Barnstaple with nylon knapsacks full of good intentions.

'Tarka!' they breathed. 'And at the Owlery Holt, no less!', and within seconds the cub's picture and location were beamed by satellite across the known cosmos, and within minutes the roads to the bridge were jammed, and within hours there was a hysterical press release from the tourist board, and within days a hotel chain was urging customers to *'Paws for a break. Get the de-tails from our webbed-site. You'll find it otterly relaxing down here in Devon. No need to fish around for alternatives. Our spa is re-eel-y the best'* – and within the week the bitch and her cub, used though they were to attention, noise and stress, had abandoned the holt which had been used by otters since the Civil War and gone to live in a drain on the edge of a housing estate.

There, for a while, they were left alone, for the kids of the estate never went outside, and the dogs were too fat to get down the bank, and from there the cub started his travels: enormous travels.

~

The young otter's great-great-great-great-great-great-great-great-grandparents had been the last generation of water-wanderers. There was no time for wandering now. The otters had to march: to be sternly mission-focused.

The water was a poor source of food, but it was still a relatively safe way to travel. So the otters saw the rivers as the motorways, and constructed their mental maps around them. But often they would leave the rivers and range the land like giant stoats – often, indeed, chasing stoats off rabbit-kills. They became as adept as foxes at breaking into hen-houses, smart as herons at pilfering goldfish from garden ponds, and canny as crows at finding partridge eggs.

Road crossings were as much a part of the young otter's education as catching big salmon had been in Tarka's day. Traditions develop quickly if your lifespan is as short as a typical modern otter's, and there were now traditional crossing places, marked by flattened otters and the daily apparition of biologists with clipboards and black bin-liners who scraped the otters up and took them off for autopsy.

The huge route marches of modern otters meant that they were far less connected to *place* than otters had traditionally been. It meant a much shallower understanding of the entwinedness of things, of the significance of the cycling seasons, and much less time for the intricate patterns that, in ordinary times, describe the movements of otters round one another. It meant that threat – a sophisticated and time-consuming form of theatre – gave way to violence. Territories, which had regulated behaviour, dissolved. So did ancient taboos about killing or badly injuring kin. Many an otter died snapping on its own entrails after it had been unzipped by a brother in a fight over a thin fish. And there were many eunuchs in Devon, for when fights happen in the water, testicles are hard to guard and easy to reach.

Our young otter had little time to learn the ropes. When he was eight months old a biologist sighed, made a note on her clipboard, and loaded his mother into a black bag.

He did not have the strength, the skills, the knowledge or the will to be a modern otter. He barely had the will to live at all. He certainly did not have the will to live as otters should.

He followed the river slowly downstream because it gave him a direction he otherwise lacked and a push which his legs and tail failed to give. When he was tired, as he usually was, he floated. He was safe in the water, though he once got a fright from a spaniel used to retrieving shot ducks from the sea. True otter hunting had long gone – and with it the real knowledge of local otters that used to be exchanged in every country pub in this part of the world – but mink hounds often found otters, and were intoxicated by the scent of their old quarry, and hard to stop.

He ate things his mother would have contemptuously

rejected: things unworthy of otters – carrion, worms, snails and crickets – though there were enough crayfish to make his dung still look like an otter's, and still smell of jasmine tea.

This ottery smell worried him. There was a practical reason for this. It meant that wherever he went he declared himself, wrongly, as a challenger to all other otters – otters with margins as slim as his own and jaws stronger than his. But there was that other reason too. He no longer wanted to be an otter at all. Or, rather, he did not want to be what otters had become. His decision to abandon modern otterdom was really an affirmation of his belief in true otterdom.

This sounds sentimental. It sounds implausibly *cognitive*. But that is how it was. And it is saying nothing more than that each organism seeks to be what it is, and tries to avoid being what it is not. There is nothing more trite or less controversial than that.

He passed under an old stone bridge, built for sheep and carts, and under the high new bridge with its notices giving would-be suicides a number to call. He started to get the nip of brine on his lips and in his eyes. The river swelled around him as if with a huge breath. He was garlanded with strips of weed, torn from a swaying field off Lundy. In his whiskers he felt big things, invisible in the brown water. His face was where he received, processed and reconstructed the world, and now, glad that his scent was being thinned by the water of two rivers and the infinite wash of the ocean, he kicked the last granules of agricultural Devon off his webs and set that face to the sea.

The tide, though it pushed him landwards when it exhaled, seemed to pull him out when it inhaled. Now, at moonrise, it took deep draughts of the heavy air of the dark woods and moors, air clinking with metallic legs and chitin plates, and a million mouths out in the sea were poised to slurp the legs and split the plates, and the otter was tugged out into this sea of gaping mouths. He turned on his back and now he could see the stars well for the first time and wondered if he could swim to them and if he could eat them.

He was far out now. Cloud covered the moon and the stars. He half remembered the womb where he had spent a secure nine weeks. It was like this, except that there there had been a pulse. But the pulse had not always been reassuring. Often it raced, and when it did, hordes of chemical messengers poured through the placenta, screaming alarm, and his paws had clenched and his heart had galloped. On balance it was better to be here in the sea. And there *was*, now that he concentrated, a sort of pulse, but this pulse was slow and steady and brought no alarming messages. He could not know that the pulse was the sigh of distant surf. He was content to lie here, look up and try to align his own pulse with the pulse out there.

And that's what he did, for an hour or so. I think he must have fallen asleep. It would not have been surprising. When he awoke, at first he could hear no pulse at all, and he thought his mother must be dead, and then he remembered. He raised his head from the water and heard nothing. Then he put his head under, and behind the clickings, grindings and hissings of all night-time seas he thought he heard the pulse again. It was very soft. He put his head in the water and held his breath. Yes, there it was, way off to his right, too far to register in his face, for the face was fully occupied with closer things and could not be re-tuned to pick up distant signals. The pulse was close enough to make him happy and far enough away to make him worried, for it had been much closer before he had fallen asleep. He set off towards the pulse.

There were no landmarks by which he could judge his

progress, but should it really be so hard to swim? And though the direction was clear, the pulse was getting fainter all the time. There was, though, now he was paying attention, another pulse off to his left, fainter still, but not receding. He changed direction and paddled towards this new pulse. After a few minutes the sea started to feel different. Paddling became easier. The original pulse, now off to his right, was still there, and still louder than the new one. Perhaps it was worth another try. So he changed course again, and this time the right-hand pulse grew quickly louder. A rip current had taken him out to sea, and by changing course he had swum out of it.

The rhythm of the pulse remained steady, but as it got louder he heard that it was more of a sigh than a thump: a grating, bubbling sigh. And now the clouds cleared and at once the moon was there and just ahead of him was a long line of surf, as far as his tired weak eyes could see, and beyond it a thin strip of sand, and, rising from the sand, low sand hills, bristling with grass.

He coasted through the surf, shook himself dry, hauled himself into a small sand bowl in the dunes – more like a flippered seal than an otter with four good land-adapted legs – curled up, and slept as if he were dead.

～

There, early next morning, he was found by someone else who had renounced their species for reasons similar to his: a hermit woman, going by the name of Beth to the very few people who ever addressed her.

Beth, appalled by the violence of a disease that could do what it had done to her beloved mother, by the passivity of a human community that could take that violence in its stride and simply send bunches of flowers and polite cards of condolence, had started to notice and be appalled at the background noise of the world: the hiss of unkindness as it corroded every surface it splashed; the chorus of brave and terrified whimpers; the whisper of slander. Once you start to notice anything, you start to notice everything. She smelt the fumes not just of resentment but also of diesel; heard the roar not only of dispossession but also of the ring road; saw not just loneliness and alienation but also the possibility of real community. So she had come to live here in the dunes, in a hut buried invisibly behind a screen of gorse, with an immediate family of two broken-winged magpies, a one-legged raven, a semi-house-trained badger, a box of grass snakes and a blind herring gull. Around her, in the dunes, the sky and the sea, were the other relatives. We're all broken, she would say. Or soon will be.

In another age they'd have burned her out of envy and bafflement. Today, instead of faggots, they tried to use planning regulations. But the regulations miraculously failed to ignite, and, peeved, her persecutors moved on to denigration, which didn't touch her at all.

'Hello, my lovely,' she said, as she knelt down beside the otter, offering him the back of her hand. He woke, and looked up, and smelt her specieslessness and so felt no fear. He let her stroke him, and she felt his ribs and the spines of his vertebrae and saw the lice scuttling for cover as she brushed back the fur, and squeezed his belly and her fingers nearly met because there was so little in there. She picked him up and he did not bite, but he looked wonderingly from his body to her hands to her face, as if he could not believe what was happening. She tucked him inside her coat and her heart started to beat for him.

It has taken about 25,000 years for wolves to turn into the

wolf–human hybrids that are usually called dogs. It is not now possible to distinguish accurately between a human and a dog; to know where one ends and the other begins. It's not merely that dogs look like their owners. They *are* their owners. Twenty-five thousand years is quite a long time, but then wolves never intended to become humans, and much of the process of trans-formation was the violent – or at least gruelling – suppression of certain characteristics of wolfishness which had been carefully cultivated by natural selection over aeons. Where two entities *choose* to become one it can happen very fast. Take the wedding service, for instance. And when two entities have no allegiance to their own kind, or actively repudiate their own kind, they can be melded very fast too. If a not-quite-wolf had met a not-quite-human, there would have been dogs within the week.

Something like that happened that week in the hut on the dunes. Shamans transform into their spiritual animals, usually after a terrifying apprenticeship involving death, dismember-ment and rebirth, and a strenuous set of rituals, often involving profound physiological stress or the use of various hallucinogenic plants. But it need not be so hard. Think of the old wise women of northern Europe who slipped quietly into the shape of a cat or a hare: I doubt they'd dosed up on henbane or psilocybin or danced round the fire until they were so dehydrated that the ves-sels in their nose leaked and sprayed the fire with blood.

I mustn't overdramatize. When the process server came ten days later bearing the latest attempt to prise Beth out of the hut he didn't see a human–otter hybrid. Beth didn't hastily reassume the form of a greying old woman in a flower-print dress out of a skip. He found Beth sitting outside with the otter on her lap, both of them smiling; two apparently distinct beings. And the few holidaymakers who left the café at the far end of the beach and walked along the tide-line, and the surfers who raised their heads like seals from their boards, saw an old gaunt woman with an otter at her heels.

Sometimes one of the holidaymakers came over to ask what sort of *dog* he was, and though they did not know why, they were on the right lines. The woman smiled and said he was a sea-hound. The best of the surfers, who were part of the sea – not separated from it by their wetsuits or any presumptions – understood what the dog was and how it really was between Beth and the otter. The really good ones were as austere and ecstatic as St Cuthbert who, after praying all night in the sea (because the sea was part of God, as was he), was warmed and dried by otters (also part of God) when he came back to shore.

The otter, like the woman, had to eat other parts of God to survive. In her early days of awakening this had troubled the woman, just as it has troubled all hunter-gatherers ever since humans discovered that they had a soul, and concluded that everything else must have a soul, too. In hunter-gatherers the problem spawned elaborate rituals of regret, thanks and reparation: in the woman it spawned an attitude and a mumbling litany of regret and thanks and reparation. That litany moved her lips as she walked along the beach – a mumbling often mentioned in statements to the authorities demanding her removal as a danger to children, public order, public morals and public health. Now she smiled, but wistfully, as the otter came out of the surf with a struggling dab in his teeth.

If something is one, as the otter and the woman were, can it become *more* one? It can. It is a great mystery, and the mystery of the rest of this story.

Here is a proof. Otters who become ordinarily attached to humans become psychotically possessive of their humans, so that when another creature, whether otter, human or otherwise, is perceived as staking a competing claim, the otter turns Othello, sinking its teeth into the competitor. But that didn't happen here.

There was no doubt about the otter's devotion to Beth. He lived up her jumper and at her heels, and at night he slept on his back in her bed, his legs in the air and his tail following the curve of her body. They came to breathe as one. He started to eat scrambled egg; she began to prefer fish. They compromised on mackerel omelettes, and ate little else. She learned to whicker and whistle; he, not having the larynx for speech, learned the significance of some human noises and signs, and beckoned with his head. His paws and his lips explored her face, and except when they walked or swam, her hands ruffled his fur. He was male, she was female. The textbooks say that any male who was affectionate to her, or to whom she was affectionate, would have his face torn off.

There were affectionate males. Dan, who was often to be found in his little boat in the estuary on a dark night when the salmon were running and their guardians were tucked up in their semis in Barnstaple, sometimes dropped in with a fish or two and stayed for a cup of tea and a witchy remedy for his warts. One-legged Sid, rat-catcher, bell-ringer and moth-collector of Braunton, came in the summer to visit his light traps on the dunes, and liked to mock Beth for being a soft touch for all animals, and liked even more being denounced as a brute. And gentle, earnest, tweedy John, who slouched along the beach feeling tragic and writing bad couplets about death in an exercise book. John came to the hut between stanzas and ate mackerel omelette gloomily, hunched and silent and looking out to sea and the oblivion he loved. Then he rose, nodded at Beth, hobbled over to her, hugged her clumsily, and stumbled out into the wind.

That hug should have been the end of him, or at least of his face. But not only did he and his face survive; he was hugged and kissed by the otter too. It was very strange. A zoology student at Exeter University wrote a prize-winning dissertation about it which came to no conclusions whatever, and so was feted for its objectivity.

The otter took to waking early in the morning, which was not like him, and undulating into the sea. There he was a different animal, every bit of him liquid, flowing in a way impossible for a creature made just of muscle, bone and blood; bending unanatomically as water winds around stone, feeling the sea fizzing into his face and from his face into his paws, and juggling the fish between his paws before biting into them and feeling their life stream into him.

He often brought his fish back on to the shore to eat them. He had a favourite rock, now crusty with scales, just above the line where the shredded weed and the wrecked birds were washed up. He saw it as a work table; a place of business, for eating was business. He could see the dogs waddling up the beach without being seen or smelt (not that they had meaningful eyes or noses, most of them), and Lundy, when it chose to be seen, and little boats dragging feathered lines for mackerel. Beth joined him here, and he ripped off and left the best bits for her, and his nose and eyes followed her finger as she pointed out the running of the waves, and the plunging of the gannets – all the way from Pembrokeshire – and the slick of oil that flattened the sea and made it look peaceful though that was the most violent part of it. And he stood on his hind legs to get a better view, weaving and swaying like an old drunk at closing time.

Sometimes she slipped into the sea beside him – the first real water she'd been in since her own amniotic sac. She did not bend as he did, but the bone spikes in her neck and back began to dissolve, and when she came up out of the surf, shaking herself, she could swivel her head as he did to watch the gulls.

The world turned, and the light drained out of the land and out of the rivers into the sea. The sea was greedier for the light, and made better use of it. The river was dark with leaves, and the light too thin to cast thick shadows from the stripped trees. But in the sea the summer still burned in the bodies of tiny things and shone in halos round the fins and gills of haddock.

The sun clung on to the roots and the sand and was clenched in the fists of the trees. Geese came from the north, and wrenched tough grass from the fields behind the dunes, thinking it luxury. At night they flew high and fast over the sea, landed in salt furrows, and watched the stars climb until it seemed they would burst out of the ceiling of the sky, and then some geese tucked their heads under their wings and swung with the waves until just before dawn, when they unpacked their heads and saw that the stars had stayed in the sky after all but had started to fall into the sea. And some geese watched all night, being the watching type, and could have told the others that there was no need to worry about losing the stars.

Smaller birds were dragged along in the wake of the geese. They looked fragile – tiny hearts humming inside weightless bone-boxes, boxes with grass-stem legs and split-seed toes and thin horn beaks full of nerves to feel the scratch and fart of sand worms, and paper wings churning the air furiously and making it like thick cream so that the birds wouldn't fall, any more than you'd sink through a pavement. They survived because they were small: when the clomping feet of the storms plonked down on the land, they escaped between the toes; when the punches of the winter landed they dodged into the space between the knuckles. When the ocean set out to break bigger, hubristic things, in its boiling wrath it didn't notice these little things scampering along the seam of the sea.

The otter played with the birds as he played with summer flies, but they disappointed him. They did not buzz round his nose, but skittered down the strand and continued to dash their heads into the beach. Beth, in her old maid's swimming costume, liked to come at them from the sea, hiding behind the surf, dragging herself the last few yards, her thin sharp hips cutting two tramlines in the sand, and then erupting among the birds. She was the least cruel person in the world, but she enjoyed their confusion; enjoyed being an event in their lives; enjoyed seeing what they did when the flock was split; wondered which of the minds – or was it all the minds mysteriously combined? – decided to wheel back and stitch the remnants of the flock together.

The otter tried Beth's game. He burst fast out of the sea, into the birds, and up to Beth, one of the birds twitching in his mouth and sand-worm juice dribbling down his chin, and Beth took the bird and kissed it and held it up to the light, wrung its neck and left it for the rats. She said nothing, but the otter would not play the game again and soon the flock's memory of death from the waves ebbed away.

Though the winter came, and the light left, it was not winter as it used to be. There were no huge white killing birds from the Arctic tundra or the silent woods of Scandinavia. There was only ever a puckered film of ice on the ponds, like the skin on Beth's evening cocoa. The otter never had to risk his life by tugging down a swan and drinking its blood. He killed a dog once – a footling, yapping, irrelevant poodle which was an offence to nature, but that was about justice, self-defence and aesthetics, not food, and he couldn't have eaten a scented, shampooed animal, as none of us should. He buried it in a rabbit hole, and after a couple of months, it smelt a good deal better.

The earth stiffened, but not to steel. The grass-tips whitened in the night, but by mid-morning were again the tired grey-green of English winter. The rooks drilled for worms in the softened earth from lunchtime to nightfall. The fleshiest surfers stayed in their summer wetsuits. Beth put out fat for the blue tits, but out of habit rather than conviction. The shore birds not only endured, which was their only job now, but thrived – which made a nonsense of many things. The red deer stayed on the moor and left the turnips and gardens alone. Bees woke before the flowers, and starved. Hedgehogs snored less deeply, and sometimes tottered from their dry-leaf nests, and round the woods, hungover with sleep, drunkenly eating the slugs that should not have been there. The fulmars did not need to fluff themselves on the ledges. Christmas bats fed on dopey Christmas moths. The dog-walkers had thin coats and no hats and in their baths, horrified, they twisted off the ticks that should have been asleep until Easter. The salmon ran up the rivers two months early, the fleas hopped in the sun on the neck of a basking fox, and a peregrine narrowed her eyes against the glare. Screaming gulls snatched ice cream from screaming children in January. Drains were blocked with unwanted soup. Streams fogged with algae. Frogs grappled ecstatically in ditches. Flowers unfurled. Snakes thawed, unwound and pushed out trembling tongues to catch the scent of an unseasonal crocus. Hedges trilled. Town cars, undercarriages scraping the tarmac under the weight of the kids and the picnic, clogged the roads down from Georgeham. There were rumours of February swallows, and before February was out a snake had climbed up the blooming blackthorn to eat a clutch of newly hatched song thrushes, the badgers had had a spring clean, the lambs were almost edible, the crows shone, the fox

cubs chewed on the rubbery bones of the year's second generation of baby rabbits, the geese were thinking of the lakes of
Iceland and wondering if they were too heavy to fly that far, the
Braunton shops sold out of buckets, spades and inflatable dinosaurs, farmers scratched their heads and rewrote their plans,
and goldfinches stretched out on ants' nests to be squirted with
formic acid.

And the sea: the old implacable sea; the sea swelled as the
bellies of the voles were swelling, but with meltwater from
ancient glaciers, and bided its time, eyeing up the woods beyond
the dunes, and the moors beyond the woods.

The otter loved it. There was plenty of amusing killing to be
done, and after the killing a shake in the surf and a roll on the
new grass. The teeth of winter had never closed in his legs or
his tail or his liver, but still he knew that the warm Atlantic
wind and the green were good. He saw white sunlight split by
the drops of the turning wave into many colours, and thought
that if white light was like that there was no end to the wonders
of the unfolding world.

But when he woke beside Beth in the night he knew she was
not well: felt it in her crimped neck and crouched in her bladder and running down the big lines on her palms. He tried to
rub some of the sun on his coat off on to her to tell her it was all
right, and she thanked him by ruffling him, but her neck and
bladder and palms were the same.

She knew that the Earth needed to rest, regroup, reorganize
and make sense of the summer; to redraft its stories in the cold as
we did when we were sane, and knew that if the big stories failed
there could be no little stories either – not that any story is *really*
little. She knew that the stories were set to trillions and trillions
of contrapuntal tunes, and that the flies and dolphins and

logarithms and principles danced, and that if the pace was too fast one dancer and then another would drop behind and then, because every proper dance needs every dancer, the dance would be spoiled by the malcoordination of even one. She felt the spoiling in her neck and bladder and palms, and pushed the otter gently aside in the night to go outside and swivel her neck and scratch her palms and try to pee the spoil out of her bladder.

It wouldn't go. It stayed and spilt out into her pelvis just as it stayed in and moved through the world, and moved into her eyes, and the otter saw it there.

He knew that the spoil would move, because everything did. Rivers flow, seas churn, prawns dash, limpets graze, rocks get wet, then dry, and lichen creeps over them, and the rocks themselves crumble into the sea and the moor. He was not troubled by worries about whether there was such a thing as an eddy in a river – the eddy being composed of different atoms every moment. He *knew* that *all* was *process*: he lived in process; caught fish in process; his defecation was process; the hairs on his legs had never lain in exactly the configuration they were now, and never would again in the history of the universe, and that would be true whether or not he licked his legs. And the *process*ion he knew was all glorious: a procession from glory to glory; from mackerel omelette to a small plaice to a slow sand eel and then back to the omelette. And since by the time he ate the sand eel he had forgotten the taste of the omelette, the omelette was new and splendid and a huge improvement on the sand eel. Then, after the omelette, the novelty of a rabbit was beyond splendour. So, circling back to old–new omelettes and new chases and new waves and whirlpools, the whole procession got better and better as his taste for splendour and omelette and sand eel and waves was honed, and so of course the spoil would be washed out of Beth's eyes and she would shine more brightly than she ever had.

Beth, long ago, before she knew what she was asking, had asked to be claimed by the land. It was a brave, terrible and very old prayer. (She had never had the nerve to ask to be claimed by the sea, but had assumed that the process of getting old would give her that nerve. That hadn't happened.)

Her prayer had been answered. For no one distinguished between Beth and the dunes. Her hair was the colour of the moonlight on the grass, her hands mottled like the lizards' backs. She had a mole on her back patterned like the beetles that clustered on the ragwort. Her clothes were heavy with sand. Most of her molecules came from a few acres round her hut, as a badger's come from a few acres round its sett. She went to Braunton once a year, on the Feast of St Michael and All Angels, for no reason she could identify. Last time she took the otter, asleep at the bottom of her backpack, and had tried not to see the pointings or hear the mutterings, and had bought a bar of chocolate, taken a bite and thrown the rest in the river. She kept the times of the dunes, and was awake at four on summer mornings and asleep by six in the evenings of the winters-that-never-are. Sometimes, her head on the ground, she thought she could hear the slow breathing of the dunes and then realized it was her own.

Now her rest was gone. She could weave no new stories, and could make no sense of the old stories about herself. She simmered in the winter heat, but no flavour came off her bones along with the flesh that was now coming away.

The otter was a good judge of flesh. Now, at night, Beth's toast-rack ribs grated against his tail. He saw that the spoil was still in her eyes; that there was more of it, and it was forming into lumps.

He did not understand this, for in this strange spring there were more fish, rabbits and flies than ever, and his own story was as sunny as the beach and the woods, and the grasshoppers were back, and he had caught a small salmon and brought it, still twitching, to Beth, who had hacked a petrol can in half and used it to steam the salmon, and they had eaten it together looking out at the hunting gannets. But Beth had jumped up and rushed off and he had heard her make the sort of sounds otter cubs make when they eat bony fish too fast, and next day there was a little pool of salmon where she had been. She melted, though not with the sun.

By high summer the dunes were an oven. The hollows filled with hot air, and there was no wind to sweep it out. Grass turned to hay in the fields long before it was cut. Ice cream ran down the children's arms before the gulls could dive for it. Sand eels, flung on to the shore by languid waves, were cooked before the gulls could find them. Families huddled under beach umbrellas to look at their phones until it was time to join the queue of traffic. Surfers cursed the children on bodyboards. The cafés doubled their prices. The gardens smelt of paraffin and charred meat. The shops ran out of beer and fans. Everyone ignored the hose-pipe ban. It was said that there was an outbreak of amoebic dysentery in Barnstaple. Some herons died of botulism. The abortion rate shot up. Youths broke beer glasses into their friends' faces. Rabbit milk dried up and because the young rabbits died underground the young buzzards died in the tree tops. Fire from fag-ends killed one thousand three hundred and forty-two meadow pipit nestlings and eighteen late cuckoos, not to mention an uncountable number of shrews, voles, mice and sheep ticks. A desperate barn owl ate his own chicks.

'It used to be the winter that bit us badly,' mused Mark the cider-maker, leaning on one of the barrels in his cider shed and watching the swallows loop in through the door and up to the beams where their lean chicks were screaming. 'Now it's the summer. It's not right.'

Beth was not right either. She tried to sleep in the day, but the heat that withered the dunes seemed to come from inside her. She rose when darkness fell, and limped down to the sea, now bent nearly double, the subdued otter at her side, looking up at her, trying to interest her in a dead dolphin or an oyster-catcher's skull or a doormat. He jumped up to nibble at her face: he could do that easily now, even when she was walking, and she nibbled him back, getting strength for a moment from his salt fishy spit and the keen edges of his teeth.

Only in the sea could she unbend, and then only at night, when the dogs had waddled back to the cars and the litter was invisible. Then she and the otter wound round one another and her guts let go of her. Then she opened her eyes under the water and saw friendly stars, and lay on her back and saw the same stars marching from horizon to horizon. The otter always had to push her back to the beach these days; had to remind her that the sea was not her home; that they had to go to the hut, for omelettes had to be made, birds' legs splinted and cabbages watered.

Back on the beach she could see no stars, and the spoiling came back inside her. I should not complain, she said to herself; nothing is hale and whole for long; we are all prey. But that sounded strained and false when she heard her voice properly, for secretly she did not want to be spoiled, and did not want to be eaten. There is only so much we can share happily, and it does not include our offal or our bones.

Spoiled or not, the world continued for the moment to spin. For most humans the spinning was like the rocking of a cradle. It reassured: it was soporific. But for Beth there was no peace and no sleep, for the spoiling of the world now grew fast inside her like a monstrous child, and her spoiled belly pushed out to meet the spoiled world of which it was a part. She felt the desperation of the child to be born and to join in with the spoiling of everything, and was too tired to resist its will and its push.

There were still omelettes to be made and legs to be splinted. The obligations of caring, as the wise well know, can stave off everything for a while, including death. Whenever she stroked the otter's head, or put his meal in the bowl, or put out fat for the blue tits, or changed the dressing on the burned hedgehog, the spoiledness retreated and the child shrank.

For a while.

On the night when, for the first time that year, there was more dark than light, Beth gently pulled back the blanket that covered her and the otter. She did not put on her shoes, but opened the door of the hut and walked out through the bowl of moonlight and into the sea, and there she lay on her back again and smiled, and her temperature was soon the temperature of the sea.

The otter was woken by the sun streaming into his eyes. He moved his tail, but Beth was not there. He slid down from the bed and undulated round the hut. No sign. The door was open. He went out. The prints of her bare feet led across the dunes and down to the sea. He followed them, stopping on every fifth print to sniff and to try to fit his prints inside hers.

The prints led into the water. The tide was coming in fast, washing the trail away; putting her traces into solution. The otter whickered; stood on his hind legs and stretched his neck to look out to sea. He turned in confusion back to the remaining prints and moved back up the beach following them. Then, understanding, he turned back to the sea.

EEL

Anguilla anguilla

Somerset Levels: 2022

She knew it was about time to die.

She had known for a while. It was a sort of decision. For the last few seasons her eyes had become mistier and the thrust of her tail slower as she jabbed out of the weed to seize the face of a tench. Leeches waved on her gills like anemones. Her swim bladder was stiff with scars from parasitic worms, her fins had been eroded by fungi, and her back raked by pike teeth.

Inside she felt an uneasiness. Something was swelling – pressing against her gut and making her strain to void. This, though she did not know it, was the ballooning of her ovaries. I don't know if her ovaries had told her that she had to die for them, or if the death wish had come first and told the ovaries to ripen. She was eighty-three years old, and entering puberty.

Dying was going to be strenuous. It could not be done in her present condition. For eighty years it had not mattered much what she ate, as long as she kept herself ticking over, resisted the earthworms squirming on hooks and the balls of wool lowered from the bridge, and had the wit to stay buried in the mud during the day, as the feathered spears that men call herons paced the side of the rhyne.

But now it was different. She needed fat for the journey to her own cemetery, and that meant killing. She set herself to the job with a determination that she'd not shown since, as an elver, she'd pushed up this river from the sea with the desperation of a sperm for an egg.

She did not alter her routine, for that would have meant hunting in the day, which would have exposed her to the heron's yellow eye, but the dark near the bridge was now frantic with thrashings and beatings and gurglings and the silent surprise of dying fish which have no eyelids or eyebrows to signal their fear. She pulled ducklings down into the night. She butted the bank with her head so that earthworms fell into her mouth. She bored into the chest of a drowned bullock and wrenched out green chunks of lung. She nibbled the once comely ankle of a depressed receptionist who had drunk a couple of bottles of vodka, taken a jump from a bridge, and rolled gently against a sluice gate among beer cans and tampon applicators.

She rooted round in the mud like a pig, nosing out swan mussels. The crack as she crushed them sent squadrons of cruising sticklebacks bolting into the reeds. One good night gave her a bellyful of younger eels. Some of them refused to die even when marinated in her digestive enzymes and squeezed by her gut, and she felt them swimming, twitching and gasping inside her through the long day.

Another female eel, old too, but younger than ours and a good deal smaller, lived in a mud cave under the overhanging bank, first carved out half a century before by the plunging feet of watering cattle and made colossal by scouring brown water. This younger female knew our eel. She had watched her nervously as the old lady worked her beat up the rhyne, across the moor, up to the mill pond, past the dissolved monastery whose monks had lived on eels and eel taxes, and back down to the scummy pool by the pumping station. Now she saw the old one's length and girth – as long as one of the solid watermen of the Levels and as thick as the thighs of their sparrow-thin wives – and saw there endurance and wisdom and a knowledge of tides, and planned (there is no other word for it) to swim in her wake towards Bermuda when the time came. So when she saw the old lady chopping and crunching, she too chopped and crunched until she too, full of roach and receptionist, started to turn into a sack of eggs.

The young one got no nearer Bermuda than the pumping station. As she idled near the surface one September dawn, jaws like bolt-croppers bit her in half and added her to the streaks of fat coursing through the old lady's body.

For three years the old eel prepared for the journey: packing her bags, padding her ribs. Her mud-coloured scales sloughed off as she rubbed against the screw that opened the floodgate, and became part of the mud. Under the old scales, her back was the black of the deep sea, and her belly was the colour of the moon, and now the sea and the moon began to rule her. She felt the gentle tug of the tide, far off in the estuary where the porpoises dawdled and the oystercatchers probed. She had known the tug all her life. Twice a day the sea had pulled her against the gate, reminding her that she'd have to go with it one day. Sometimes an ambitious front of salt water, pushed by a wind that, like the eel, had formed in the mid-Atlantic, forced up and through the gate, and made her gums shrink from her teeth in fear and excitement. Once or twice in her time winter storms had washed small green shore crabs into her pool, and as she chewed them she'd known again (though it wasn't quite remembering) the press of glistening bodies against hers, and the crash of surf.

That last summer she harvested, sweeping the river in disciplined strips like the rowdy red machines cutting grass for silage on the fields around. Used to hunting with her nose and to decoding the trembling of water, she now took to chasing like a gaze-hound, for her eyes, getting ready for the dark Atlantic troughs, had ballooned along with her ovaries, and now filled half her head, and could see tails and fins where once she knew only scent molecules or knots of ruffled water.

The call of the sea and the beckoning of the moon grew stronger as September drained the heat of the moor and the cows huddled under the blackthorn.

The rains came, washing more mud into the river, and cooling it further. Even the eel's new eyes strained to see through the haze. The pool by the gate became more and more like the sea. It had curdled in the sun; now it swirled and there was no light and it became a mystery even to the eel. And suddenly – it happened one night – the eel was a sea creature again.

But the time was not yet right. Though the river was fuller than it had been all year, it was not yet desperate to spill itself into the sea, and after all those years the eel and the river shared a point of view about the right time of things. And it was too light. The moon was full, and the moon had to be empty before the eel would move. A full moon would scorch her huge eyes, for moonlight has a way of trickling down to the bottom of a river, and the moon, the sea and the eggs of females have some sort of accord, in eels as in humans.

So the eel waited, grabbing only occasionally at drifting things, for she was on the starting blocks, set on travel and sex and death.

When the moon waned the tension turned to tremors that rippled the length of her body, making the pool tremble. Yet no rain came. That month and the month after, families basked, chattered and spread out their picnics, and the cattle clacked over the baked soil to stand in the shrunken river. They hadn't known nothing like it, said the farmers. Not for a fair while, anyhow. The eel, seeing the river drop, slotted herself back into her old groove at the bottom of the pool, wafted mud over her back in case an otter should look too closely, and the pool was still.

Somewhere, deep in the eel's body, she knew that the race was on, that she was yet to join it, and that her eight decades were about to look pointless. But stronger even than this voice of urgent despair was the logistical voice: Wait for the water: wait for the dark.

The dark came again. The moon was a sliver of ice behind the abbey, but still the water ran clear and low. Soon the moon would fill again, but the river had a lot of filling to do. The nights were hot and full of flies – the great-great-great-grandchildren of the midsummer flies, who should not have existed now, let alone be breeding as they were. The farmers cursed and sweated in bed, and started to feed the silage meant for winter because the sun had burned off the autumn grass. Small birds, which might have flown to Africa, saw no need to face the moody gods of the Mediterranean or the dust storms of the Sahara, and stayed chittering in the hedges.

But in the east the sky was tightening. Inside the clouds, droplet ground against droplet and the clouds itched blue and hummed and sparked, and the clouds stretched and fattened and headed for the sea as the eel wanted to do. And late one night, as the farmers drank up the last of the cider and mopped themselves and murmured that it was hellish close, lightning split an oak on the moor from its top to its roots, firing it, cremating a nest of wood mice and a couple of jackdaws, waking the heron, and announcing the unburdening of the cloud.

For a week the eel had known the approach of the storm. Had heard it as a drawl in the water and a muttering of the frogs and felt it as an itch down her flanks. At the smashing of the tree she shook herself out of the mud cocoon and swam to the surface, where the first few signal drops had started to pucker the pool.

She convulsed at each crack of lightning, as if she was plugged into the sky. She reared out of the pool, shivered her fins in the rain and flopped back. A fat worm, washed out of the bank, dropped past her nose. She let it go. She would never feed again.

It is never the rain that falls on you that makes the difference. It's the rain that falls many miles off. In a few hours the river rose fast as the water streamed off the baked earth in the tangled uplands, as impermeable for a while as a glazed teapot. But soon the pot began to crack, and if you'd put your ear to the ground you'd have heard a popping and a clacking as the soil stretched, and if you'd had feet like a blackbird or a bill like a woodcock you'd have felt the stirring in the earth: the click of centipedes and the scratch of earwig legs. The trees shook off the summer and took deep draughts of the water before the streams filled at last.

For three days after the lightning the rain fell. On the night of the third day, at around midnight, a pulse of cold new water came down the river and into the rhyne, slapping against the gate by the pumping station. The eel had felt it coming from a mile away and had readied herself, twitching in the scum at the top of the pool, huge eyes burned by the tiny moon.

The eel rose on the pulse, lunging up and out, but the water was too low. Her nose hit the metal gate with a thud, she fell back into the pool, and her jaws opened and shut in a silent scream. Again and again she tried, but – like most of us – she was trapped in the place she'd lived. Her nose was soggy with the bruising. Her throat was raw where it had scraped over the screw. Still she tried, as the moon sank and the sun climbed, and then the pain in her eyes was too much and she sank back to the mud cleft.

There were more pulses that day. The land above seemed to clutch the water as tight and for as long as it could, and then to tire and release its grip, and at each pulse the eel lifted her head out of the mud, and felt the burning, and let it fall again.

In the night she banged again against the gate. Again; again – until there was blood in the floodwater and the eel, tasting it, was excited for a moment out of habit, until she knew that it was her own blood, and remembered that she didn't eat any more.

Long past midnight, as an owl killed a vole on the bank, the eel knew that the water was falling again.

Something very old but very odd then happened. The eel swam down the rhyne to a place where the bullocks watered. The bank there was broken down by their feet. The eel, pushing her tail on the mud, rose into the air as if from a snake-charmer's basket and slumped heavily into the meadow. Turning west, she slithered through the grass by the side of the rhyne: swimming, her skin and gills pulling oxygen from the air as before they had pulled it from the river; finding the same essential resistance from ryegrass and dock and cow-pats and thistles as she got from water. Down the rhyne side, under a gate, between the legs of bemused cows, round the edge of a hawthorn hedge, past the pumping station with its gauges, pipes and wheels, and back, in a slimy glissade, into the water – the water, this time, of the river, not the rhyne. On the map the river imitated the eel's body, curling, sliming, insinuating its way to the sea.

Eighty years ago the eel had made the journey up this river from the sea as anti-aircraft guns pumped steel into the sky at German bombers grinding up the Severn estuary towards Bristol, and shrapnel rocked down through the clouds of migrating elvers.

It had been a freer world then. There had been no barriers,

gates or sluices to stop or slow the young eels, no turbines to mince them, and few nets, for most of the elvermen were at war. But now the whole river was a series of holding pens – or, if you prefer, an almost impossible steeplechase. No elvers had reached the eel's pool for fifteen years. Very few got to the gentle murmuring village on the river just below the pool, where the river flowed so slowly between a glass-blower's workshop and a curry house that it was hard to see that it flowed at all – and indeed it often flowed backwards, away from the sea.

The eel, cow dung caked on her silver belly, came to an iron gate. The gate was designed to divert water, in time of flood, out of the river and down long ditches, so reducing the rising damp in a breezeblock housing estate, stopping the river depositing in the local allotments the fertilizing silt for which the ancient civilizations prayed, and encouraging the gardeners to apply nitrogen from the garden centre instead.

It could not be said that the eel had a memory – as we know memory – of her ascent all those years ago. But she did know, as she drummed her bruised head against the new gate, that this was not how it was meant to be; that she and the world had once flowed as the river once flowed.

The eel had another three hours of darkness. The water lapping at the gate was three inches lower than it had been the previous night. This was a struggle against principalities and powers; against the very way the world was. Eels had spent the last hundred million years in the water, and now the water had failed.

She turned and swam back up the river. There was no weariness in the turn, nor in the thrash up the bank and on to the footpath; just the manic energy of the last chance; the fight for the last breath. She would not trust the water again until it tasted of home.

Along the path she went, through a field of barley stubble, watched by transfixed rabbits and baffled crows. Into a ditch, over a mound of builders' rubble, under a roundabout in a children's playground, across a road – causing a milk lorry to slew to a halt and making the driver rub his eyes and wonder what had been slipped into last night's beer – through a flock of uninterested sheep, and a wood where she was watched by a buzzard who sometimes took snakes but wasn't at all tempted to have a go, past a sleepless dog-walker – sending a wheezing, bow-legged bulldog cringing into the nettles, and his owner to a long and futile course of psychotherapy – and along the high street of a small town, supermarket receipts sticking to her throat. A postman backed against a bookie's to let her pass, his jaw hanging. A policewoman at the end of the night's patrol saw her slide down an alley, picked up her radio and was about to bark an incredulous report to control when she thought that if she wanted that promotion she'd better not. Through a kitchen garden, leaving a highway of slime over the cabbages and lunging at an outraged cat, and out on to a plain of rough grass which gave way to mud.

Now the eel could feel the sea on her thick grey tongue and in the panting pores of her skin. The mud slid to the brown water, and the eel, for once running with the grain of the world, did too.

The southern Sargasso Sea, North Atlantic: April 1939

The Sargasso, blue, clear, warm, very salty, dead still, 15,000 feet deep, nearly sterile, but festooned with chandeliers of hanging weed, is held in a bowl made of a colder and still deeper sea which drops four miles to a desert floor. The floor is crossed, in terrible loneliness, by ancient things that make their own light, and by twisting hungry machines with teeth. Everything here eats the light of the sun they will never see; light coagulated in the muscle of eels and the bones of whales.

The bowl, like most bowls, is made by turning. The Sargasso is held in place, and held still, and its saltiness held, by a gigantic clockwise swirl – the compromise reached when hot and cold currents collide. This sea, like everywhere and everything, is the way it is because of the way that places far distant from it are.

A female eel, who started her life here in the middle of the Zulu War, and who had lived her life in a gloomy pond in the Tuscan hills, and who had built her huge body from cherries and frogs, smooched and clamped with a small taut male from the easy, brackish waters of a Libyan estuary. He spurted five times over the twenty minutes of their relationship. In the blue twilight under the weed she seeped, and so our eel began, rising as her spent parents sank.

She looked like a thin glass leaf, brittle and veined. Like leaves caught in an autumn eddy, many of her siblings would never escape the ocean vortex. But somehow our eel drifted to the edge of the plughole and was spat into the grey cold to the northeast. She rocked along, deep under the storm and sun, relying on the current for her future, for she had no real motor of her own, and if she had, she would not have known where to steer.

Perhaps once a week over the next three years another leaf-eel passed within a mile of her, hanging in the half-light. Of the leaves that had started to drift, most had withered and fallen. But the size, the loneliness and the dark of the sea were her friends.

The open Atlantic was more dangerous and more bounteous than the Sargasso. She gorged on the plankton that billowed like smoke from the marine trenches. In that first summer of life, she was gargled by an inflamed rocky throat half a mile down and might have ended there. But she was swallowed by a viperfish which, swimming fast to the surface, was itself taken by a small shark. The shark tore its prey, and out of the viperfish's stomach, in a haze of blood, squid limbs and digestive enzymes, floated the eel.

She inched away from the Sargasso when the wind and the sea chose, and went back when they chose. By the winter she was a hundred miles from her parents' bones. She was now 25 millimetres long, and sometimes part of the spray in the west Atlantic rollers – just a big lump of plankton forming part of the wave's long arc.

One wild February night a wave started by a humpback fluke off Tierra del Fuego and grown by Bermuda to the height of a cathedral picked up the eel as it wallowed in a trough with a shoal of bruised and seasick sardines, hurled it, curled it, and buried it in a column of bubbles fifty yards deep. And there it caught the current which had streamed resolutely north-east since the last Ice Age – a current that saw the mighty wave as a flippant child – and was drawn into its cold salt paunch and travelled on.

There were no seasons down here. The mountains and valleys were far below. There were packs of hunters with spangled sides and needle teeth, and others ash-white with writhing heads, but the sea was big and the eel was small.

She grew, though. By the time it was summer in the world above – the world of wind and rain and shearwaters – she was five centimetres long. In July a dog snapper saw her, and saw the eel's own prey twitching in the thread of her gut, and the grey sea through her head and flanks, and had opened his mouth to make an end of her when a bigger mouth yawned out of the abyss and sent him streaking to the surface.

Our eel spent this second summer of her life in the centre of the Atlantic. She swung between continents. There was no real swimming. The Atlantic was a big amniotic bag: she had the same control over her location and fate as a human embryo has over hers. She had eyes, but they were pointless except as place-holders for the eyes that would one day lock on to worms and shellfish.

The time of her (limited) autonomy drew closer. But there was a determined campaign against it. If a baleen whale six hundred miles off the Azores had pulled just one more gallon of brine over his whalebone combs, she would have been broken. If the wing of a storm petrel had been aligned just one degree further to the south, its foot would not have trailed quite so early in the wave and its beak would have closed on the eel. If she had not been pushed under by the wake of an Argentinian grain boat, a tubenosed bird, unknown to the museums and the textbooks, would have had her.

Her eyes started to work, and one February she saw, far below her, another eel of her species – a male, this time from a stagnant mill pond in Provence – swimming fast back to the Sargasso. He was no threat to her now. He had no functioning gut, and an appetite only for sex and death.

The sun rose and the sun set and the sea ground down the land, and by the end of the eel's second year much more of the planet was in solution than it had been when she was born, for the sea always wins. The eel did not care about the sun except that it charged the organisms that kept her own motor turning, or about the storms, except that they snatched away the feet of birds and drove her nearer to or further away from the shore or made no difference at all.

When she was two years old things very, very slowly began to change. In the world at first, rather than in her own body. The world that was the water round her body started to fill with life and food. The sea became shallower. The currents became bumpier and more erratic. There were eddies as the currents bouncing off the approaching continents hit one another and glanced off, spinning. The tubenoses were joined by packs of raucous gulls who couldn't dive but had fine eyes and fast hooked beaks.

When the seabed started to climb towards the land, the eel started to shrink. She became shorter. Her head, compared to her wispy little body, looked monstrous, and her anus, as if pulled by the gravitational force of the head, crept forward. Her teeth looked less like a wolf's. In a few weeks she was a tenth of her former weight. You could still see the sea through her. She was a wraith, the colour of sea mist.

The ocean might have turned her right at the junction of Africa and Europe, taking her through the tidal race of Gibraltar and spewing her into the Mediterranean. She might have fattened on fish heads and *cannoli* tossed into the Grand Canal, or become the legend of a Turkish lagoon, or terrified children in Bulgaria, or grazed all her life on the little green crabs of Algiers before being tangled in the propeller of a refuelling gunboat, or climbed high into the brown velvet hills of the Alpujarra, plucked flatworms off rocks and snatched chorizo from goatherds' fingers, or swum through the Hellespont, the Bosphorus and the Black Sea, and been hauled out of the Danube and clubbed and smoked and eaten with horseradish, or lived a quiet life in a Thracian drain.

But the ocean hurried her on, slamming the doors to all these destinies. It swept her north, along the low, long strands of Portugal, with palm bows from the Gambia and a U-boat engineer from Stuttgart. It might have spooned her into a rotting freighter listing under the peeling rococo of Lisbon. She might have smelt the sweet water of the Douro or been hooked inland by one of the jagged headlands of Galicia, or choked on a toad in the Basque country. But instead she swept on into the heaving trenches of Biscay where, if she'd had much of a stomach, she'd have felt queasy alongside the mackerel that were too seasick to eat her. Even now she might have been spun east and slithered into the Dordogne or up the Loire to face more systematic fishermen than the shambolic amateurs of Somerset. She had no say. She went where the sea's caprice sent her, on past Finisterre. Here there was yet another crossroads in the sea.

She might have swirled east into the Channel, perhaps ascending the Seine and finding a cave under Notre Dame and growing sleek on daytrippers' sandwiches; or felt the shock of goosestepping boots on the road by the Rhine, or been speared with a pitchfork under a Dutch bridge, or been persecuted by water bailiffs in the chalk streams of Hampshire, accused of eating trout fry; or been chased and chewed by a grim Fenland otter, or deafened by Baltic depth charges, or burrowed into the mud over the ribs of a longboat in a Norwegian fjord; or streamed to Iceland under the waistcoats of puffins and wormed over a black beach into a bath of hot sulphurous water from the centre of the Earth.

But for some reason or none these doors too were shut, and she sailed sedately on between Scilly and Land's End. Off Newquay a whirlpool from a whale's tail nearly pushed her into a current flowing westwards, which would have taken her to a mid-Atlantic limbo – a place of no possibilities. But instead, for some reason or none, the sea turned her back towards the land; past Hartland, off Lundy, back into Bideford Bay (where, tasting the Taw and the Torridge, she almost joined the procession

through Barnstaple and into the coombes and moors of Devon).
Here she was disgorged by the two rivers back out into the last
of the Atlantic before it became the little brown Severn sea; up
the Exmoor coast where peat-water rank with red deer musk
welled out among armadas of human turds from Bridgewater
and the slicks from a winged bomber that never made it back to
Germany.

In Bridgewater Bay there was a great gathering. A squirming ball of life was hardening just beyond the mild brown
breakers. A million streaks of protoplasm twitching and
travelling – though they didn't know where – with the determination and the look of gigantic sperm. They had heads, and
in each head the nerves bulged out into a distinct brain – which
didn't do much except register the difference between salt and
fresh water, and turn the streak towards the fresh. The motions
of the body – the flailings of the tail, the jerkings of the body
away from encircling cod and pollock and the teeth of eels
seeking to eat their own children – were directed not by the
nerve-bulge but by sparking circles of impulses through the
spinal cord without, often, even a note sent to the bulge to tell
it what the body had decided to do.

The eels at the core of the ball – those safest from the teeth
outside – were hardly distinct entities. They were more like the
brains of the ball itself. Their movements shuddered out
through the ball and became its movements.

The eels were waiting for something, but had no idea what.
Indeed, they had no ideas. They were part of each other and
part of the sea, and if there was a will it was diluted among the
million jelly-bodies and by the muddy brine.

The brine, not the eels, made the decision. It had always been
that way. For all we know, it may be that way with us. But with

the eels hanging in the warm soup that had spilled from the bowls of Herefordshire and Gloucestershire it was very obviously so. For gathering slowly out of the channel was a wave the height of an eel-fisher which squared its shoulders and lowered its head and drove between Wales and England as if to split them. Most of the wave pushed up towards Gloucester, shoving flatfish and whale ribs into the mudflats of the Forest of Dean, but a rebel franchise switched east, making for the misty lowlands of Somerset.

This eastbound wave picked up the shimmering ball of glass eels and rammed it down the throat of the river.

The eels now knew something about themselves for the first time: the wave gave them *will* even as it took from them all possibility of contradicting it. They knew now that they had to go up – up with the rolling water; up from the smell of kelp and the slippery sides of sunfish, to the smell of grass in the dung of cows, and meadowsweet and reeds and iron flakes from the rivets of floodgates and the white medicinal tang of the willows that wept into the water of the Levels.

Had they been waiting for this moment – the moment of ascent? The biographical facts, seen from the distance at which all humans see all eels, insist that they had. Yet it cannot be – at least if to wait means to expect, or to choose (when other options are possible) to defer action. There was no room in heads so small for such a complex notion: no space for the dense entanglement of the sizzling neurones necessary to generate the idea of a present and a future and to identify and inhabit the gap between them. They had been swept on since the Sargasso, and had recently begun wrigglingly to contribute to their own sweeping, but they remained *swept* creatures, as perhaps we all are. But there was a plan afoot – a plan of echoing ancientness and audacity, and, etched clearly into that plan, in the arcane calligraphy used by evolution for its blueprints, were the words *Wait for the tide.*

Even in the last moments of the waiting that she did not know she was doing, the purpose that our eel did not know she had was almost frustrated by a pollock that might have been knowingly waiting. The pollock drove into the ball of eels. A dozen dribbled from its fat lips. Our eel, near the top of the ball, burst blindly up into the air and dropped back into the sea. Ever after, the taste of air meant alarm, and she avoided air when she could, as wise humans avoid hospitals. She might have been a confident, mid-water eel, taken in her teens by a heron. The pollock made her a reclusive mud-eel, and preserved her and slowed her clock.

The ball unfurled. Eels streamed up the sides of the mud cloud that humans call the river. Until now, each hour of travel had been a *tendency* to go east or north. Now, with a thrill that registered even in those rudimentary nerve knots in the paper-thin eel skulls, there was *direction*. It was like the difference between Brownian motion and a speeding arrow. I have never felt this, but our eel did.

Out in the bay the eel had sensed a lightening in the water as the salt was diluted by the river and her own body became heavier. Now, in the river itself, she fiddled amateurishly with her buoyancy controls, and sometimes sank out of the eel-stream towards the mud, where mouths gaped.

The eels, for the moment, were the life and death of the estuary. Other prey stopped trembling for a while as birds and fish hovered and stooped on the eels. An early spring butterfly, not yet in control of its wings, landed on the river and trembled there between the worlds, its wings wicking up water. Had it not been for the eels, it would have vanished into a fish maw, and the molecules of its antennae would have been reallocated as the building blocks of a repaired pectoral fin. But in their frenzy the fish ignored the trembling, and the butterfly shook off the water and shuddered into the meadow, where it founded a long and august dynasty, for a quirk in its genes made its off-spring hateful to birds.

A starving otter, disabled by a festering pitchfork wound and unable to hunt, lay in the eel-stream, facing down-river, his mouth open, and the eels poured into him and down him, pro-pelling themselves so the otter hardly had to swallow. They saved him, the wound healed, and he lived to kill many more eels.

In the cottages on the riverside they knew the eels would run on this day. Most of the men were away at the war, and the eel-harvest was left to boys and old men. They dragged huge nets on frames from the sheds, pulled last spring's dried weed out of the mesh, the women darned the holes, and the nets were borne down to the banks in sacramental procession. For though the eels would end up in buckets and fish-cakes and spread on the potato patch as fertilizer and fed to pigs, and though the eels had always come, there was, even for the grossest and most modern human inhabitants of the Levels, nothing industrial or inevitable about the run. The fishermen knew nothing of the voyage of the eels; of the confounding of contingencies that had brought each one of the millions to the river. Yet they sensed the same wonder and power thrilling along the mudbanks as they felt in their own arteries at night, and knew that they were killing holy things, and that the killing should be clean.

There were two main skills in elvering. The first was to know when. On this day that wasn't hard. The river slowed and stopped, the sea puckered and boiled, and then the river turned on itself and flowed uphill, and then the eels came.

The second was to know where. This was mainly about how to avoid being drowned. Many an elverman, in his passion to get his net far out into the crystal ribbon of bodies, felt the mud close over him.

Our eel joined the north-bank ribbon. Her shape and her sinuations were determined by the press and shiver of the bodies all around her. There was no thought – if there ever had been thought of anything – of feeding. Nor even of survival. *Up-ness* was all. To her right was the son of a female who had lived in an abandoned drainpipe in the Vlatava and a male from the Golden Horn; to her left the son of a compulsive cannibal from Bulgaria and a pale Icelander with a taste for guillemot liver; above her the daughter of an ample Umbrian yeoman and a straggling bootlace from a Lithuanian well; and below her the spawn (destined for long tenure of a Mendip mill pond) of the legendary terror of an Alpine lake and an undistinguished suburban eel from a Hertfordshire lake full of prams.

All slid over the rim of a net and survived the day. Most around them did not. Many were fried alive in margarine. Others drooled out of the nets like jellied rain and dried to a crisp, or were ground under boot heels. The thin ration-book omelettes of Bridgewater were fishy-stiff that night, peppered with black pinpoint eyes.

But our eel went on. The river wound through fields where buttercups streamed in the tide. Tadpoles in the flooded footprints of cattle were caught up and carried off in the eel-stream. The river passed under a bridge crossed by a khaki convoy of grumbling trucks and grumbling men, and the grumbles dripped into the water and made it sour.

The tide turned and the river flowed once more towards the sea. Some of the eels slowed and were carried back downstream;

some sought refuge under the arches of the bridge; many found refuge in the mouths of tench, roach and eel.

Those that continued met a fork. Those on the left bank took the left fork; those on the right the right fork. Except our eel. She relinquished the left bank, swimming insanely through the subway-crush of bodies and across the grain of the river to join the right-bankers. I don't know why. I don't know if the question 'Why?' means anything here.

The right-bankers, by and large, did well. The right fork split into remote backwaters, far from roads and rods, where the feet of watering cows pushed worms into the river, perch fry hung in jittering clouds in mid-water, and occasional clumsy hedgehogs rolled down the steep banks and floundered hopelessly for a few hours before letting the river close over them.

Most of the left-bankers died in the summer when, near the headwaters, a farmer emptied a tank of sheep-dip into the river, clearing the invertebrates, and so everything in the food chain above them, for ten miles downstream.

Our eel saw out the war as a local vagrant, winding from bay to bay, carcass to carcass, sewage pipe to sewage pipe, fish to fish, mussel to mussel. She learned where the farmer's wife emptied bins into the river, where the frogs bred, and how to wrap her tail round a root to make it easier to pull moorhen chicks down into the dark. She learned to overcome her distaste of the light on summer days when the mayflies were hatching, for the bodies on the water (papery, contemptible things, not worth the effort of a gulp) brought other bodies with hearts and livers and muscles. When her jaws grew strong from all the bodies, she learned to crack the horse mussels whose siphons waved above the mud. She became a horse mussel specialist, and so there were barely any seasons for her. The pronouns I've used for 'her' now became meaningful. She had started life gender-neutral and spent years as a hermaphrodite, possessing male and female sexual organs. By the time the Allies occupied Sicily, the male organs had withered.

Other eels were few and dangerous. She backed from them, barking silently. She had no need of companionship; only of food. The war mattered mainly because the rubbish bins were emptier.

There were adventures of a sort.

In the fifties boys, fishing for roach, reeled her in. She curled round the line. They yanked the hook from her mouth, taking with it a lump of gristle and leaving her teeth on that side forever askew, and tried to crush her head with a brick. But she twisted so fast that the brick landed, I'm glad to say, on a boy's foot instead. Then, in revenge, they tried to cut off her head, but she slipped through their hands like air and slid through the nettles back into the river.

In the sixties the propeller of a small boat churned up the riverbed where the eel was resting, hacking a groove into her back. She healed, though ever thereafter she preferred to make her final dashes in a clockwise curve.

In the seventies the river was dredged so that the farmers could be told that something was being done about flooding. Our eel, along with fifty tonnes of homes, ecosystems and arguably ensouled creatures, was scooped into a mechanical shovel and dumped into a barge. She was out in minutes, pushing blindly through the mud until her nose hit the side, and then up and over, and splash.

In the eighties the river itself was sliced up like a cucumber. It was again to do with flooding; with the need to control, divert, hold back and release. It meant the walls, fences and gates to which humans, in their fear, are so attached, and by which they are so constrained – while thinking themselves the constrainers.

The river and the sea could have chosen not to comply; could have chosen to wash the works away with one shrug of their watery shoulders. They chose not to do so. They could bide their time, and as I write they are still biding their time.

The slicing turned the river into an archipelago and its inhabitants into islanders. The river stopped flowing as it had since the last Ice Age, and so did genes. Brothers mated with sisters, and monstrosities and glorious innovations erupted into the water. There were fewer strangers from the hills and the sea, but the river now bred its own strangers.

By and large it didn't bother our eel. The monstrosities tasted the same. Few eels now came through her patch, but they had never been a big part of her diet, and she was now invulnerably big. Of course she had no interest in reproduction. That would happen, if it happened at all, on the other side of the Atlantic. A part of her – an old part – was indeed glad (if gladness has a place in a head that sharp) to be spared the brackish twice-daily reminder of inevitable travel and extinction.

In the nineties, though, the new stillness became deadly. The fields bordering our eel's slice of the river had been looked after by an old farmer. He died. His son was impatient of the slow old ways. He fulminated with ideas and calculations, and flushed slurry into the river.

Lots of life loved it. The river bloomed with bacteria, algae and weed. And the blooming – the purr of all the mitochondrial motors – choked the river, suffocating all but the favoured.

The eel managed well enough for a while. There was plenty of floating carrion. But eels are quite fastidious animals – they much prefer fresh meat – and though she did not grow thin, she grew nauseated, and one night she swam upstream (it's always *up*, for eels, at the pivotal moments in life, until the very end) until she thumped against the gate which penned the next slice of river in place. She sniffed at the cracks where the water came through, and, as she was to do many years later, pushed up on to the land, through the cow parsley and the timothy, round the gate, and back into the river.

This too was putrid, though less so than the old slice, and she carried on up, through water thick as custard, weed-strands cutting like wire into her gills, until the water again started to be watery. Here she could have stayed, but the disgust was on her now, and when a rhyne let into the river she shook the river from her scales, climbed the bank by the gate, and dived deep into the pool.

Here she stayed, as I have told. I do not know if an eel can be content, but there was a lack of adventure, and that must have been pleasing. Here too there were mussels, and hence no seasons and hence no years.

In the new millennium a disappointed lad, down from London for the weekend, went out by the river to escape his loving mother, dosed himself up on cocaine and urinated into the river, right where the eel was resting. Eel skin is very porous – it's one of the ways they exchange gases – and the eel got a fair dose. It nearly killed her. For a day and a night she convulsed, throwing up the latest crayfish, straightening out like an iron rod, knotting herself so tightly that her tail went blue, and shaking in time with the aspen on the bank above. This was the chance of a culinary lifetime for the speckled pike that lived in a hall of reeds and had hung hungrily in mid-water for ten years, eyeing the fillets on the eel's back. But the eel's movements were so alarming, so diseased, that the pike missed his chance. He was lucky.

After a torrid day and night the spasms calmed, the eel unknotted and resumed her usual curve, and the boy went back to the office.

Hunting became harder. The river was not what it had been. But barring a general sloth and a few scabrous malignancies on her skin, both caused by living in mud fouled by discarded batteries, the eel lived a fairly untroubled life.

She did not know, and would not have cared, that throughout the wider world eel populations had fallen. The few people who cared used words like 'catastrophic' and 'devastating', but it is not clear whether they meant by that anything more than that there were very, very many fewer eels than there had been.

The oceans were hotter. The old currents did not behave as they had, and millions of young eels never broke out of the vortex of the Sargasso. Many that did escape were swept back and died where they were born, or were carried north or south and never knew sand or shingle or mud, knew only salt water, perished in the deep green Atlantic, and became part of the trenches that form the valleys between the towering mountains of the sea.

The glass eel runs were an ooze, not the gush they had been. But the riverside nets weren't left to rot. Far from it. Scarcity changed the rules and the people. There were no more elver omelettes in the cottages. It would have been like swallowing diamonds. The Far East had an inexhaustible appetite for eel, eels could not be bred, and the eel farms in Japan and China that fed the restaurants where live eels pouted in the tanks all had to be supplied with glass eels captured in the wild. So evolution populated the riverbank with a brand new race of men in sharp suits, with bundles of cash in their briefcases: men who couldn't handle a net but were deft with the laws of supply and demand and deft at dodging the well-meaning laws inhibiting elver exports. Private jets with refrigerated tanks now waited for the tide in the brown sea. River to pig, river to pan, and river to garden compost – though brutal and wasteful – now seemed honest and organic beside the cynical chains of middlemen. The eel world of Somerset had smelt of slime, sweat and cigarettes: now it smelt of duty-free aftershave. The commercially important meetings were no longer in dark laybys, but in offices with mirror windows.

If an eel wriggled past the pillars of the free market and on into the labyrinth of water-roads, water-lanes and water-tracks beyond the drag of the tide, its chances of maturing were still remote.

It might be chewed by a turbine and spat out as paste, fail to find a way past the many dams and weirs that constipated the river, or starve because pesticides had wiped out the invertebrates on which the whole biological infrastructure was built. Weakened and dozy, it might more readily fall prey to a cormorant or heron. The screech and thud of boat engines disabled its anti-predator mechanisms.

If, against all the odds, it silvered and its gonads swelled and it turned its nose to the sea, it would swim into a tight net of new dangers. Silver eels, unlike the yellow eels they had been, made good eating, and the same men who had tried to kill them as elvers were waiting for them in the estuary, with different nets, on the stormy nights when the waters had risen and the sea had called. Many a silver Somerset eel, just five thousand miles from fulfilment, ended up beech-smoked and shrink-wrapped in Knightsbridge.

But that was far from the worst of it. At the best of times the journey was arduous. The unforgiving sea, and natural selection herself, expected first-rate condition. No modern eels are in that condition. Many are thin, without the reserves necessary for the fasting race to the Sargasso. Many are infected with a nematode, introduced by imported eels, which damages the swim bladder and makes buoyancy hard to control. Many are weakened by lifelong doses of pesticides and metals. Many of the toxins are held in the fat – relatively harmlessly until the fat starts to be burned. When the eel starts to mobilize the fat, the poisons start to work, sending their physiology haywire. If the eel itself survives the poisoning, its reproductive system might not. The pesticides of the twentieth century might block or corrupt the sperm or egg production of the twenty-first.

~

Our eel, travelling alone and deep on her way to her death, missed the nets in the bay. The Almighty Himself, say the big game hunters, looks after a lone rogue male, and He looks after lone rogue females too. Had she been caught, mind you, she might have looked after herself, ripping the mesh and taking a finger or two with her before they managed to put a spike through her head.

She steered out under the fringe of surf with the same certainty about her course as she had when she was certain she had to eat. The direction was a mere fact: not a matter of judgement. She was not triangulating from the boom of waves on a cliff, the scratch of pebbles on a strand, and the fizz of a submarine fountain. She was not reading currents or following the scent trails of generations of eels along the sea-road. She never surfaced to take bearings from the stars. She had a compass in her head – magnetized particles that swung with the Earth's own field and made the eel's nerves itch – but a compass is no good without a map. The eel was going to her death, and death was a place, just as a euthanasia booth is a place. It was death that had the distinctive smell. Sex had exactly the same smell. Memory had no part in the journey. She had no memory of death, sex, Lundy, Land's End, Biscay, the great mountain ranges off the coast of Senegal, or the waves a thousand feet down where the swordfish played.

She tunnelled through the dark cold, untroubled by honking ships and their cargoes of vanities. Anyone seeing her would have seen the seriousness in her swimming, and been ashamed of their own flippancy.

She knew when she was approaching the end because the water was suddenly saltier and she had to adjust her buoyancy. The sensation was like walking from an energetically air-conditioned supermarket into a red-hot street. It brought a new kind of knowledge of her imminent extinction – the new, focused kind of knowledge that comes when a particular letter from the hospital drops through the letterbox.

She began to see movements in the sea around her – convulsions which hardened into shapes. All were desperate and doomed. As she swam on, all was wooing and coupling. The wooing was varied. No one there had seen it done, done it before or would do it again. Temperament and life experience showed. Eels who'd had hard, fighting lives showed few niceties. They shoved and flaunted. Brazenness paid. There wasn't much time. Eels wound round each other as candyfloss round a stick.

Our eel could take her pick. All the males were far younger

and far smaller, and at some level supposed that her great length and girth meant that she was a super-fit survivor – and that her offspring would be robust craft in which to set afloat their own chance of posterity.

So they massed round her, a hundred metres down in the thick clear sea and the last of the light, ignoring the drowned beetles from the Guyanese rainforest that rocked down past them.

She was too tired for romantic nuance. She swam on, and let the males fight it out between them, and went with the most persistent: a Turk. They locked for twenty minutes; she leaked, he spurted, and thousands of hopeful embryos were adrift under the canopies of weed and plastic trash.

She and the Turk had never met, but each, on one view, was the whole point of the other. It is purpose that keeps everything alive. They now had no purpose. Life ebbed out with the purpose, and they sank together into the dark, three miles down, into the graveyard they shared with all eels.

Their embryos sailed on. The winds and the currents were kind. The embryos stretched into tiny eels.

It is not clear what happened then. A complete DNA sequencing might help. At six months old, as everything seemed to be going well, almost all of the young eels shrank, shrivelled and died. I myself am inclined to blame the coolants from a box of capacitors that was dumped in the rhyne in the 1970s.

I say that *almost* all the young eels died. It may be that one or two lived to feel the drive to up-ness in a river somewhere, and perhaps lived, too, to leak, spurt and die in the deep blue.

I hope so.

EPILOGUE

This book of stories is over, but the story is not.

We have been in this book to some dark places – made dark by human selfishness, negligence and power. But individual humans are not – though governments generally are – selfish or negligent. And individual humans are powerful. Individuals are far, far more selfless than they are selfish. The kindness of strangers is the rule. We all long for relationship, though we often express that longing in stammering, dysfunctional ways. We all long for better stories to tell ourselves about ourselves. We know that the readily available, synthetic stories are pathetically inadequate, and we know that for a story to be a good story it has to have others in it – for monologues are desperately dull and biologically illiterate. We know, more and more, that our defining and dignifying and downright pleasurable relationships are not only with humans but with non-humans too.

I'm very hopeful of a better story.

AUTHOR'S NOTE

I've tried to get the science right. Or (this being a book of stories, with a fair bit of speculation), at least not wrong.

In the course of researching the book I've read hundreds of scientific articles and a mountain of books, and talked to many very patient experts.

I can't list the articles and books, but if anyone wants to read just one book or article about each of the seven non-human animals depicted, I suggest the following:

Fox: David Macdonald, *Running with the Fox*, Unwin Hyman, 1987

Orca: John K. B. Ford, Graeme M. Ellis and Kenneth C. Balcomb, *Killer Whales: The Natural History and Genealogy of* Orcinus orca *in British Columbia and Washington*, University of British Columbia Press, 1996.

Mayfly: George F. Edmunds Jr and W. P. McCafferty, 'The Mayfly subimago', *Annual Review of Entomology* 33: 1, 1988, pp. 509–29. In my story I've conflated several species of mayfly. This article considers many species.

Rabbit: Ronald Lockley, *Private Life of the Rabbit*, Corgi, 1976.

Gannet: Bryan Nelson, *The Gannet*, Poyser, 2010.

Otter: James Williams, *The Otter*, Merlin Unwin, 2010.

Eel: Steve Ely, *The European Eel*, Longbarrow Press, 2021.

As for *human* – well, there's a question. Certainly one book won't do. Perhaps flip between *Mein Kampf,* Jackie Collins at her most banal, and a biography of Boris Johnson on the one hand, and *The Matter With Things* (Iain McGilchrist), Homer, *Lear*, Plotinus, *The Story of my Heart* (Richard Jefferies), *Zorba the Greek* (Nikos Kazantzakis), *The Rubaiyat of Omar Khayyam* or Peter Matthiessen's *The Snow Leopard* on the other? I've had a hubristic stab myself at saying what sort of creatures I think humans are (*Being a Human*), but my approach will be too direct for many: there's a lot to be said for the idea that we only see anything worthwhile (such as dryads or oncoming vehicles or novel mathematical proofs) at the edges of our vision, and that shy things like badgers and identity and the real nature of anything bolt if you walk straight up to them.

I'm very conscious of following in an august and intimidating tradition of nature writing. My main debts are obvious: to Henry Williamson (the otter story starts with the opening words of *Tarka*, and many of the dystopic scenes are updated versions of Tarka's adventures), Richard Jefferies, 'BB', Peter Matthiessen, Brian Carter, all the American transcendentalists and, more recently and in a wholly different genre, Carl Safina.

In this book I'm often very rude about humans. It would be wrong, though perhaps understandable, to read that as misanthropy. Yes, I'm disappointed in humans. But one can only be disappointed if one has an expectation. My expectations of humans, despite everything, are glorious. If the *Imago Dei* isn't a theological fact, it's at least a good summary of how we *really* are when all the political and nationalistic and corporate and commercial crud is sluiced off.

So although I've raged and fulminated, I've never for a moment despaired. It's my generation and preceding generations who've besieged and raped and trussed and poisoned the world. Those guilty generations and their ways are about to be as extinct as the dodos we casually and greedily clubbed. Those who follow have seen what selfishness does to rivers, forests and our souls, and they'll not be so stupid as to follow in our footsteps.

ACKNOWLEDGEMENTS

Writing any book is an act of conscious or unconscious plagiarism. I've plundered many sources and hounded many people, and I can't acknowledge or thank or apologize to them all – partly because I'm often unaware of what I've stolen, and from whom.

But I know that I'm particularly grateful to:

David Abram, Patrick Barkham, Michael Brown, John Butler, Rachel Campbell-Johnston, Peter and Laura Carew, Mark Cocker, Helen Conford, John and Margaret Cooper, James Crowden, Steve Ely, John and Nickie Fletcher, Jay Griffiths, Duff Hart-Davies, David Haskell, Caspar Henderson, Ben Hill, Geoff and Mandy Johnson, Helen Jukes, Paul Kingsnorth, Ed Lake, Andy Letcher, John Lister-Kaye, Iain McGilchrist, Nigel McGilchrist, George Monbiot, Helen Mort, Gregory Norminton, Keith Powell, Jill Purce, Colin Roberts, Martin Shaw, Merlin Sheldrake, Rupert Sheldrake, Claire and Mike Smith, Chris Thouless, Hugh Warwick, Emily Watt, Jimmy and Melanie Watt, Kate and Mark Weil, and Mark and Sue West.

Alex Christofi, my amazing editor at Transworld, believed in this strange book from the start, and hugely improved it. As ever I'm in awe at the wisdom and kindness of my agent and friend Jessica Woollard. Gillian Somerscales' masterly copy-editing made the book far better than it was.

Everyone in my family has been part of the adventure of thinking myself into the heads of these animals. They've stoically swum across lochs, frozen in furrows, crawled through rivers, sat motionless and bored rigid in hides, been drained nearly dry by midges and endured both my absence and (what's often worse) my grumpy, distracted presence. You're superb, and I can't thank you enough.

It no doubt seems a whimsical pose to thank the non-humans who've contributed to this book. But I'll have to risk it. You invited me into your homes – or at least tolerated me there. I've swum, crept, climbed, slept and even tried to fly among you. I've peered at you through binoculars, cut up your dead bodies to see how you're made, listened in to your most intimate moments, and misunderstood you. Thank you for bearing with me.

NOTES

Preface

p. xiii, 'what an animal is feeling': Carl Safina, *Beyond Words: What Animals Think and Feel* (Macmillan, 2015); Charles Foster, 'Anthropomorphism: faulty thinking or useful tool?', in Andy Butterworth, ed., *Animal Welfare in a Changing World* (CABI, 2019), pp. 177–81.

p. xvi, '"the pathos of actuality in the natural world"': Ted Hughes, *A Memorial Address. Henry Williamson: the Man, the Writings* (Tabb House, 1980), pp. 159–65.

p. xvi, 'two of the three books she would take to a desert island': Arlene R. Quaratiello, *Rachel Carson: A Biography* (Greenwood, 2004).

p. xvi, '"any careful reader"': Stuart Cole, 'The animal novel as biopolitical critique: Henry Williamson's *Tarka the Otter*', *Interdisciplinary Studies in Literature and the Environment* 26: 3, 2019, pp. 540–69 at p. 542.

Orca

p. 34, 'torture it until it did tricks': It is true, though, that dolphins have been recorded behaving towards other species (notably porpoises) in ways that are undoubtedly unpleasant for those animals. This includes toying with them before killing them. It is difficult to know what to make of these reports. We should be slow to call it callousness – let alone sadism. It may be that playing with injured or doomed animals in ways that look cruel to us serves some useful function – for instance in teaching young dolphins how to hunt a porpoise.

Charles Foster is a *New York Times* bestselling author whose work has been longlisted for the Baillie Gifford Prize, short-listed for the Wainwright Prize for nature writing, and won the Ig Nobel Prize for Biology and the 30 Millions d'Amis Prize. He is a fellow of Exeter College, Oxford, and has particular passions for Greece, waves, the Upper Palaeolithic, mountains and swifts.